3-MINUTE
PRAYERS
For
Teen Girls Journal

180 Devotional Prayers

Published by Barbour Books, an imprint of Barbour Publishing, Inc., 1810 Barbour Drive, Uhrichsville, Ohio 44683, www.barbourbooks.com

Our mission is to inspire the world with the life-changing message of the Bible.

Member of the
Evangelical Christian
Publishers Association

Printed in China.

3-MINUTE
PRAYERS
for
Teen Girls Journal

180 Devotional Prayers

Margot Starbuck

BARBOUR BOOKS
An Imprint of Barbour Publishing, Inc.

Introduction

How can a young person stay on the path of purity?
By living according to your word.
PSALM 119:9

When life feels full—with school, friends, church, family, work, sports, and other activities—it can seem as if there are no extra minutes to spend in God's Word. And yet your busy life is exactly why it's so critical to carve out time to be still in His presence. You can actually pause to hear from God, to be nourished by His Word and by His presence, in just three minutes a day.

- Minute 1: Read and reflect on God's Word.

- Minute 2: Pray, using the provided prayer to jump-start a conversation with God.

- Minute 3: Reflect on a question for further thought.

This guide is different from an in-depth Bible study. It is meant to nourish you from God's Word so that you can savor the sound of His voice hour by hour. Use it as a springboard to continue talking with God, and listening to Him, as your day unfolds. May these scriptures and prayers be reminders of God's faithful presence with you, in every moment.

Loving Like You Love

"A new command I give you: Love one another. As I have loved you, so you must love one another. By this everyone will know that you are my disciples, if you love one another."
JOHN 13:34–35

Jesus, I hear the words You spoke to Your first followers and the words You speak to me: *Love one another.* I confess that although I long to live faithfully, my flesh gets in the way of me loving my family, loving my friends, and loving the world that You love. But You've shown me what love looks like. I learn how to love when I peek into the Gospels and see how You loved rich and poor, adults and children, saints and sinners, male and female, Jews and those who weren't Jewish. And because You equip me, I commit to loving others with Your love today. Amen.

THINK ABOUT IT:
*Who in the rhythm of your regular daily
life is God calling you to love?*

....

....

....

....

....

....

....

....

Living As One Who's Accepted

Jesus said to her, "I who speak to you am he." . . .
So the woman left her water jar and went away into town
and said to the people, "Come, see a man who told me
all that I ever did. Can this be the Christ?"
JOHN 4:26, 28–29 ESV

Lord, sometimes I fear that if people really knew me—if they knew my history, my thoughts, and my fears—they would reject me. So I show the world the version of me I think they'll accept. But inside I'm hungry to be received and loved exactly as I am. I see Your generous face smiling upon a woman who was rejected in her community. And I see You smiling upon me. Lord, fill me with Your gracious presence so I can live as one who is known and loved by You. Amen.

THINK ABOUT IT:
What parts of yourself do you prefer to hide
from others? Can you offer those to Jesus?

When I Hurt, God Is On My Side

You've kept track of my every toss and turn through the sleepless nights, each tear entered in your ledger, each ache written in your book. If my enemies run away, turn tail when I yell at them, then I'll know that God is on my side.
PSALM 56:8–9 MSG

Lord, You know the hurts—the little ones and the big ones—that I hold in my heart. You've kept track of every bruise, bump, and tear. And although the deceiver hisses that You do not care for me, I am convinced that You are on my side. I am comforted by Your presence and grateful for Your care. God, thank You for receiving all of me, even my tender places. Amen.

THINK ABOUT IT:
*What are the hurts from your past
that are known only to you and to God?*

Committed To Purity

How can a young person stay on the path of purity?
By living according to your word. I seek you with all my heart;
do not let me stray from your commands. I have hidden your
word in my heart that I might not sin against you.
PSALM 119:9–11

God, You know exactly what I'm up against as I commit myself to live faithfully to You. You know what other students are talking about and what they're doing on weekends. You know how culture bombards me with temptations. And You know how I can be tempted to rationalize my words and actions. God, I am seeking You with my whole heart. I believe Your Word strengthens and empowers me to avoid sin. Be my Helper today. Amen.

THINK ABOUT IT:

Is there a particular scripture that
emboldens you to avoid sin?

Obeying My Father In Heaven

He replied to him, "Who is my mother, and who are my brothers?" Pointing to his disciples, he said, "Here are my mother and my brothers. For whoever does the will of my Father in heaven is my brother and sister and mother."
MATTHEW 12:48–50

God, I am convinced that loving my family well is one of my foremost assignments from You. So I'm on it. Help me to love them well. I'm also aware that my first allegiance is not to members of my family—especially when they do not know You, love You, or obey You—but it is to You. Father God, in life and in death, I belong to You. As I seek to live a life of love, one that is faithful to You, be my number one priority and Lord. Amen.

THINK ABOUT IT:

Is there a place in your life where you need to listen to the voice of God over the voice of others?

....

....

....

....

....

....

....

....

....

Using Words For Good

A gentle answer turns away wrath,
but a harsh word stirs up anger.
PROVERBS 15:1

Lord, although I want to honor You in all I do, I confess that this is difficult when anger bubbles up inside me. When someone messes with me at school, when they say things that aren't true, when my siblings annoy me, and when I disagree strongly with my parents, I want to lash out in anger. But Your Word challenges me to choose my response, my volume, and my tone carefully. My words have power—either to fuel a fire of angry rage or to de-escalate conflicts. God, help me use the power of my tongue for good, using my voice to turn away wrath and sow seeds of peace. Amen.

THINK ABOUT IT:
Is there a particular situation—on the bus, in the car,
or early morning in the bathroom—in which you're
often tempted to fire off angry words?

God Is Working For Good

We know that in all things God works for
the good of those who love him, who have
been called according to his purpose.
ROMANS 8:28

Lord, when I look at some of the painful or difficult situations in my home, in my larger family, in my community, and in Your world, it is sometimes hard to find hope. When I see the ways that so many suffer, it's difficult to find meaning in the chaos. But Your Word reminds me that I don't see all that You see. I trust Your promise to work behind the scenes for the good of those who've been called by You and who love You. God, although I can't make sense of all I see, I put my trust in You today because You are good and You are faithful. Amen.

THINK ABOUT IT:
Where in your life is it hard to
see what God is up to?

Spending Myself For Others

"If you do away with the yoke of oppression, with the pointing finger and malicious talk, and if you spend yourselves in behalf of the hungry and satisfy the needs of the oppressed, then your light will rise in the darkness, and your night will become like the noonday. The LORD will guide you always."
ISAIAH 58:9–11

God, You have made plain what delights Your heart. And You've promised that when we care for the most vulnerable, You are pleased and Your favor is with us. Lord, help me to be a faithful servant who loves You by loving others. Open my eyes this week to notice those who are hungry and those who are oppressed—both those who walk the halls at school with me and those around the globe who are known intimately by You. Equip me to respond faithfully, in Jesus' name. Amen.

THINK ABOUT IT:
What is one tangible need of others to which God has already been opening your eyes?

Sin Be Gone

He does not deal with us according to our sins, nor repay us according to our iniquities. For as high as the heavens are above the earth, so great is his steadfast love toward those who fear him; as far as the east is from the west, so far does he remove our transgressions from us.
PSALM 103:10–12 ESV

Father, sometimes my sin feels sticky—like gum on my shoe. Maybe it's a sin that feels too big for You to forgive. Or one that I commit and confess to You again and again. I'm tempted to believe that those sins are still clinging to me. But Your Word promises that the sins I've confessed to You are *gone*. They've been completely removed. Today I hold on to that truth. Lord, thank You for Your grace that is bigger than I can imagine! Amen.

THINK ABOUT IT:
What sins has the Lord forgiven that the deceiver tries to throw back in your face?

....

....

....

....

....

....

....

....

God Redeems My Sin And Brokeness

"Neither this man nor his parents sinned,"
said Jesus, "but this happened so that the
works of God might be displayed in him."
JOHN 9:3

Lord, the idea that first-century people assumed that a man had been born blind because his parents had sinned, or because he'd sinned, seems like such antiquated thinking. It almost seems absurd. And yet at times part of me believes that some people are responsible for their own suffering. Or even that I am responsible for suffering that I don't and can't control. Yet Your Word reminds me that You are redeeming a broken world. So I offer You my hurting places, my broken places, and my sinful places so that Your power may be displayed in my life for Your glory. Amen.

THINK ABOUT IT:
What situation in your life is God
longing to redeem right now?

God Has A Plan For Me

I know the plans I have for you, declares the Lord, plans for welfare and not for evil, to give you a future and a hope.
JEREMIAH 29:11 ESV

God, some days it feels as if the future stretches out in front of me, but I can't see what it looks like. Some of my friends have a clear sense of what they want to study and what job they want to do one day. But when adults ask me what I want to do or be when I get older, I don't know for sure. Help! Today I take comfort in Your promise that You have a plan for my good. And that is enough. Today I take a deep breath and place my trust in You. Amen.

THINK ABOUT IT:
What are some practical things you can do to place your trust in God's plan?

Being A Friend In Hard Times

A friend loves at all times, and a
brother is born for a time of adversity.
PROVERBS 17:17

God, I thank You for the friends whom You have placed in my life. I receive my friends from church, from school, and from my neighborhood—and maybe even faraway friends from camp or from a town where I used to live—as good gifts from You. It's been easy to love my friends when we're having fun, and when we're thriving. But I ask You to teach me how to love my friends well when their lives are difficult: when they lose a loved one to death, when their parents are separating, when they're forced to move, when their sibling is ill, or when they face other challenges. God teach me to ·be that friend who is faithful in adversity. Amen.

THINK ABOUT IT:
How can you love and support a friend
who is facing adversity right now?

Being Made New

If anyone is in Christ, the new creation has come:
The old has gone, the new is here!
2 CORINTHIANS 5:17

Lord, I thank You for Your promise that anyone who is in Christ is being made new. Because that's me, God! And yet, when I look at my life, I recognize so much of the old self still hanging around. I notice the ways I act when I'm in a bad mood. I see how I can treat people poorly. I recognize the ways I'm loose with my language. And I'm aware of the ways I'm tempted, daily, to sin. But because I trust in Your promise, I offer myself to You today, so I may be *made new.* I know I can't make myself into a new creation, so I trust in the work of Your Spirit in my life. Amen.

THINK ABOUT IT:
What one particular area of your life right now
would you like to relinquish into God's care?

....

....

....

....

....

....

....

....

....

You Promise To Answer

*"Call to me and I will answer you and tell you great
and unsearchable things you do not know."*
JEREMIAH 33:3

Gracious Father, I thank You that Your Word assures me that You see me, You hear me, You know me, and You love me. God, I confess that sometimes when I pray, I feel like I'm talking to the ceiling. It's hard for me to believe that my little prayers are reaching Your ears. And yet I hear You inviting me to pray, and I believe, deep inside me, that You are listening. Not only do You hear, but You also promise to answer me. God, that is hard for me to wrap my mind around! When I pray, teach me to listen for and to recognize Your still, small voice—and sometimes loud one—that answers my prayers. Amen.

THINK ABOUT IT:
*When have you noticed, or been aware of,
God answering your prayers?*

Armored Up

*Stand firm then, with the belt of truth buckled around
your waist, with the breastplate of righteousness in place,
and with your feet fitted with the readiness that comes
from the gospel of peace. In addition to all this, take up the
shield of faith, with which you can extinguish all the flaming
arrows of the evil one. Take the helmet of salvation and
the sword of the Spirit, which is the word of God.*
EPHESIANS 6:14–17

Lord, I believe that You send me into the world as an agent
of Your new kingdom. Today, I close my eyes and visualize
myself donning the armor You provide, wearing Your protection: a belt, breastplate, boots, shield, helmet, and sword.
I am fully equipped to be Your person in the world because
You've equipped me with truth, righteousness, readiness,
faith, and Your mighty Word. God, I'm fully clothed, and I'm
ready to slay! Amen.

THINK ABOUT IT:
*What piece of armor do you anticipate
you will most need today?*

Love Covering Over Wrongs

Hatred stirs up conflict,
but love covers over all wrongs.
PROVERBS 10:12

God, I thank You that You know the name and face and heart of every person I will meet this day. You know which ones love me and have my back, and You also know which ones are likely to attack, wound, or hurt me or others. So I offer every interaction to You, God. Teach me, especially how to love those whose words and behavior are unlovely. Dispel any hatred in my heart, so that I might be a vessel that channels Your great love for them. May my love function like beautiful paint that covers an ugly graffiti wall, obliterating any hint of wrong. Not in my strength—obviously!—but in Yours, and to Your glory. Amen.

THINK ABOUT IT:
In what relationship will you need to depend
on God's help, and God's love, today?

Recognizing The Thief And The Life-Giver

The thief comes only to steal and kill and destroy; I have come that they may have life, and have it to the full.
JOHN 10:10

God, You are teaching me how to notice and recognize the voices that whisper words into my heart and head. When I have a thought to compromise, to lie, to binge, or to sin, You help me recognize the voice of the thief—who comes only to steal, kill, and destroy. And when I notice a thought inspiring me to offer love, to practice generosity, or to share joy, You help me recognize the voice of Jesus—who came to give abundant life! Thank You for Your Spirit who helps me distinguish between these voices and empowers me to choose Your holy way. Amen.

THINK ABOUT IT:
Is there a common refrain that you hear the thief whispering in your ear? A lie about you or about others?

....

....

....

....

....

....

....

The Power Of Surprising Love

If your enemy is hungry, give him food to eat; if he is thirsty, give him water to drink. In doing this, you will heap burning coals on his head, and the LORD will reward you.
PROVERBS 25:21–22

God, You know the enemies I'm facing right now. You know the people in my life who tear me down instead of build me up. I need Your help, and I thank You for Your clever and holy strategy to defeat them! You haven't given me a weapon of violence, but one of love. And You promise that when I extend love and good gifts to my enemy, I am *winning*. Today I will take You at Your word, and I will confound my enemy with love. In Your name and to Your glory, amen.

THINK ABOUT IT:
Who is an enemy in your life right now—who probably doesn't look like anything like an awful arch villain—whom God is calling you to love?

The One Who Truly Satisfies

Jesus declared, "I am the bread of life.
Whoever comes to me will never go hungry,
and whoever believes in me will never be thirsty."
JOHN 6:35

Father, everything within me hungers for life that really is life. And yet I regularly fill my heart, mind, and body with that which does not satisfy. I fill my ears with a constant stream of music; I fill my eyes with media feeds, shows, and movies; I fill my body with whatever tastes good and makes me feel good. Forgive me, Lord. Feed me with Yourself, for You are the only thing that satisfies my hunger and my thirst. I feast on You and on Your Word, and I am finally full. Amen.

THINK ABOUT IT:

With what are you tempted to fill your ears, eyes,
and mouth, hoping you will get quick relief?

"Fear Not, For I Am With You"

Do not fear, for I am with you; do not be dismayed,
for I am your God. I will strengthen you and help you;
I will uphold you with my righteous right hand.
Isaiah 41:10

God, I thank You that there is no moment of my life—past, present, or future—in which You have left me alone. In every hurt, in every joy, in every disappointment, in every surprise, *You are with me.* God, impress this transforming truth upon my heart and mind. When I'm taking tests, when I'm playing sports, when I go to the doctor, when I sit in church, when I hang with my friends, You are strengthening me and helping me. God, thank You that You never leave me nor forsake me. Amen.

THINK ABOUT IT:

If there was a moment in your life when you felt
abandoned, can you pause and return to it, seeking
God's faithful presence there with you and for you?

Serving Like Jesus

Who, being in very nature God, did not consider equality
with God something to be used to his own advantage;
rather, he made himself nothing by taking the very
nature of a servant, being made in human likeness.
PHILIPPIANS 2:6–7

Every voice around me, Lord, is lobbying me to do more, achieve more, play more, and win more. And I confess that I'm tempted—on application essays, at parties, and in interviews—to make myself appear to be more than I really am. And yet, in Your Word, I am relieved of the pressure to seem big and important. Instead, imitating Jesus, I can aim to be smaller by serving others the way He did. Father, give me Your heart to imitate the posture of Jesus by stopping to serve others, in Your name. Amen.

THINK ABOUT IT:
How will you make yourself smaller this week
as you choose to serve others the way Jesus did?

Reconciled To God And Others

"If you are offering your gift at the altar and there remember that your brother or sister has something against you, leave your gift there in front of the altar. First go and be reconciled to them; then come and offer your gift."
MATTHEW 5:23–24

Lord, I want to honor You by living well. I want to worship You with my whole heart. And yet when I have sinned against others, I cannot love You with my whole heart. When I've hurt someone in my family, or when I've said something unkind to a friend, I cannot love You like I want to. So quicken my mind to see if there are any against whom I've sinned. Open my eyes to notice from whom I might need to ask forgiveness. And give me the courage to humbly confess and ask forgiveness, so that I might be right with them and with You.

THINK ABOUT IT:
With whom do you need to reconcile because of some offense you've committed?

....

....

....

....

....

....

....

....

God Shoulders My Worries

*"Can any one of you by worrying
add a single hour to your life?"*
MATTHEW 6:27

God, when I start worrying—about schoolwork, about my commitments, about the future—I feel so alone. I carry this heavy burden of worries that only stresses me out. And yet when I listen to the gentle words of Jesus, I'm reminded that You care for me. You already know the things I'm worrying about, and You invite me to trust You with them. Just as You care for the birds of the air and the flowers of the field, just as You meet their needs, You meet my needs. I can see that worrying doesn't change one thing! Good Father, today I release my anxieties, my concerns, and my worries to You. And because I trust You, I receive Your gentle comfort.

THINK ABOUT IT:
*Is there some recurring worry, spinning in your
mind, that you can release to God today?*

Death Does Not Win

"Death is swallowed up in victory." "O death, where is your victory? O death, where is your sting?" The sting of death is sin, and the power of sin is the law. But thanks be to God, who gives us the victory through our Lord Jesus Christ.
1 CORINTHIANS 15:54–57 ESV

Lord, I struggle to understand the power of death in the world. When I see tragedies in the news, or when someone I know has died, I wrestle to understand *why*. When someone's life is cut short, it feels as if death has won. But You promise that, in the end, death does *not* win. And when I look at the crucifixion, death, and resurrection of Jesus, I know that it is true. God, even though I don't fully understand, I trust that You are the Great Redeemer. Amen.

THINK ABOUT IT:
*Where does it appear as though
death is winning or has won?*

....

....

....

....

....

....

....

....

....

Speaking To God Throughout The Day

Rejoice always, pray continually, give thanks in all circumstances; for this is God's will for you in Christ Jesus.
1 THESSALONIANS 5:16–18

God, I thank You for the assurance I have that You are with me and for me. I confess that too often I zip through my day with little thought of You. Forgive me. God, I want to notice Your presence with me throughout today. When I eat with my family, when I spend time with my friends, when I work on assignments or at my job, when I encounter strangers on the street, I want to recognize You in every one of those moments. And Your Word invites me to welcome You into each one by praying continually. God, help me to converse with You in my heart—speaking and listening—throughout this day.

THINK ABOUT IT:
Is there some kind of a reminder—a ring or bracelet, a temporary tattoo, a string on your finger—that will trigger your mind to pray to God continually?

Act, Love, Walk With God

*He has shown you, O mortal, what is good.
And what does the LORD require of you? To act justly
and to love mercy and to walk humbly with your God.*
MICAH 6:8

After You delivered Your people out of Egypt, Lord, they strayed from Your ways. And like a loving Father, You yearned for them to return to You. You even made it plain to them what You were asking them to do: to act justly, love mercy, and walk humbly with You. Father, although I wish I were better than they were, I recognize my heart in theirs. And I hear You calling me to honor You with my life in the same way. So embolden me to be a person who acts justly. Soften my heart so that I love mercy. And teach me what it means to walk humbly with You. Amen.

THINK ABOUT IT:

*As you consider God's threefold invitation
into "what is good," what do you believe
God is calling you to do today?*

Pleasing Just One

Am I now trying to win the approval of human beings, or of God? Or am I trying to please people? If I were still trying to please people, I would not be a servant of Christ.
GALATIANS 1:10

Lord, You know my heart. And You know how tempting it is for me to want to please people. I want my parents to be proud of me. I want my peers to like me. I want teachers, bosses, and coaches to think highly of me. And those aren't bad things! But when my need for human approval trumps my longing to please You, I am missing the mark. First and foremost, I am a servant of Christ. And today I commit my heart to please You above all others. Be my Helper, in Jesus' name and for His sake. Amen.

THINK ABOUT IT:
When do you notice your desire to please people interfering with your commitment to please God?

God Meets My Needs

Keep falsehood and lies far from me; give me neither poverty nor riches, but give me only my daily bread. Otherwise, I may have too much and disown you and say, "Who is the LORD?" Or I may become poor and steal, and so dishonor the name of my God.
PROVERBS 30:8–9

God, You are my faithful Provider, and I trust You to meet my needs. I confess that when I feel like I don't have what I think I need, I spend a lot of time and energy thinking how I can get it! And when I'm honest, I admit that there is a lot I want that I really don't need. You know my heart. God, I believe that You are my good Provider, and I trust that I don't need everything I want. Above all, I want to honor You. Amen.

THINK ABOUT IT:
Is there a "need" in your life right now that only God can meet?

....

....

....

....

....

....

....

....

Making New Friends

Make friends with nobodies;
don't be the great somebody.
ROMANS 12:16 MSG

God, I thank You for the crew of family and friends that You have given me. They are a gift and a blessing from You. God, I also want You to open my eyes to the ones whom this world marginalizes. Show me the people in my school, in my community, in Your larger world, and even at my church who are overlooked and undervalued. Help me to notice those from different cultures, with different abilities, the ones who are "other." Give me Your eyes to see them, Your heart to love them, and the commitment to enter into real friendship with them. Thank You, in advance, for the gifts they will share with me. Amen.

THINK ABOUT IT:
Is there someone you can think of, right now,
whom the world overlooks and God loves?

Honoring God With My Body

Do you not know that your body is a temple of the Holy Spirit within you, whom you have from God? You are not your own, for you were bought with a price. So glorify God in your body.
1 Corinthians 6:19–20 ESV

God, I give You thanks for the physical body You have given me. I know it's not *perfect*—in either its appearance or its function—but I believe that You knit me together and that my body is *good*. Voices around me try to convince me that it is mine to use as I please: eating whatever I want, drinking whatever I want, smoking whatever I want, and behaving however I want. And yet I also hear Your kind, gentle voice reminding me that my body is *where You live*! Teach me what that means and empower me to make choices that honor You. Amen.

THINK ABOUT IT:
What is God saying to you today about how you can better honor Him with your body?

The Ones Jesus Loves

When Jesus reached the spot, he looked up and said to him, "Zacchaeus, come down immediately. I must stay at your house today." So he came down at once and welcomed him gladly. All the people saw this and began to mutter, "He has gone to be the guest of a sinner."
LUKE 19:5–7

God, You know what my life is like. You know the pressures to be among peers who are popular, who are smart, who are socially savvy. And You also know the pressures I face to avoid being seen with those who are on the margins, who are awkward, who are looked down upon. And yet You made a beeline toward people like Zacchaeus who were avoided by those in their community! Today, Jesus, give me Your heart for those around me who have been marginalized. Amen.

THINK ABOUT IT:
Who needs to know God's steadfast loving presence through you today?

Winning When Tempted

*The devil said to him, "If you are the Son of God,
tell this stone to become bread." Jesus answered,
"It is written: 'Man shall not live on bread alone.'"*
LUKE 4:3–4

Some days, Jesus, I feel as if the devil is on my back. I feel as
if he is near and he is tempting me. And You know what that
is like. I take comfort in the knowledge that You faced the
enemy, just as I do. And when I keep my eyes on You, I can
see my way out of the bind. When You were tempted, You
didn't depend on Your own willpower. No, You were empowered by God's Word. That was Your source of strength, Your
superpower. Today, Jesus, remind me of Your Word so that,
like You, I remain faithful to our Father. Amen.

THINK ABOUT IT:
*What passage of Scripture is most
useful to you when you are tempted?*

Making God's Name Known

Give praise to the LORD, proclaim his name; make known among the nations what he has done. Sing to him, sing praise to him; tell of all his wonderful acts. Glory in his holy name; let the hearts of those who seek the LORD rejoice.
PSALM 105:1–3

God, You are faithful. You have done so much good in my life and the lives of others. And so I long to tell others of Your faithfulness. God, equip me today to share news of Your goodness with others. Help me share with a friend in need how You've changed my life. Help me remind a family member that You are always faithful, even when we can't see what You're up to. And help me share with someone in need the reasons why You can be trusted. Strengthen me today to tell all the wonderful things You have done. Amen.

THINK ABOUT IT:
*Through what act of faithfulness can you thank God—
and perhaps even encourage someone—today?*

My Perfect Father

"Which of you, if your son asks for bread, will give him a stone? Or if he asks for a fish, will give him a snake? If you, then, though you are evil, know how to give good gifts to your children, how much more will your Father in heaven give good gifts to those who ask him!"

MATTHEW 7:9–11

Father in heaven, I believe that You gave me parents to show me what Your love is like. Sometimes they reflect for me Your steadfast, faithful love. Other times, though, they fail to love me the way You do. But You assure me that Your love is of a higher order and that You delight in giving good gifts to those who ask You for them. Well, that's me. I am asking You to send the good gifts You have for me. Amen.

THINK ABOUT IT:
What request are you making of God today?

Praising God With My Mouth

Come, let us sing for joy to the LORD; let us shout aloud to the Rock of our salvation. Let us come before him with thanksgiving and extol him with music and song. For the LORD is the great God, the great King above all gods.
PSALM 95:1–3

Good Creator, You are the Maker of all that is, and—graciously!—that includes music. God, You know the notes and chords and sounds that I pipe into my ears every day. You know what makes my foot tap and what makes my whole body dance. I receive music as a good gift from You. And, God, I also want to return my praise to You in song. I sing to You, and I join the chorus of the faithful who thank and praise You with melodies! You are the great God, and today I open my lips to praise Your name. Amen.

THINK ABOUT IT:
What are some of your favorite songs that help you praise God?

I Have What I Need

"Why do you worry about clothes? See how the flowers of the field grow. They do not labor or spin. Yet I tell you that not even Solomon in all his splendor was dressed like one of these."
MATTHEW 6:28–29

Jesus, You are wise. And when I listen to You teaching Your first-century followers about what it means to trust Your Father, and ours, I hear echoes of solid truth for my own life. When You exhort Your disciples to worry less about scrambling after clothes, food, and shelter, I hear You speaking to me! And even though my daily physical needs are met, I surf online shopping sites for my next outfit, I keep thinking about that yummy pint of ice cream in our freezer, and I noodle on how I want to redecorate my room. But today, Lord, I trust You as the good Provider for all I need.

THINK ABOUT IT:
How has God already met your daily needs today?

God Is Near To Me

Lord, you have been our dwelling place throughout all generations. Before the mountains were born or you brought forth the whole world, from everlasting to everlasting you are God.
PSALM 90:1–2

God, I long to be in Your presence and to experience Your nearness. And Your Word reminds me that You have been the dwelling place for Your people for centuries. You have invited us to live with You. And so as I look around my bedroom today, or as I walk through my school's hallways today, I know that You are there with me! You really do dwell with me. In Jesus, You made Your home among women, and men, and children, and today You live with me. Thank You for holding me close. Amen.

THINK ABOUT IT:
In what physical place, whether in your home or outside of it, do you feel closest to God?

You Lighten My Load

"Come to me, all you who are weary and burdened, and I will give you rest. Take my yoke upon you and learn from me, for I am gentle and humble in heart, and you will find rest for your souls. For my yoke is easy and my burden is light."
MATTHEW 11:28–30

God, I thank You that You notice when I'm tired. You see when I'm overwhelmed. And You care that I am weary. You know every burden I bear—at school, at work, at home—and You offer me respite. You invite me to come and be with You, and You offer to shoulder my burden alongside me. As I picture You beside me, I can feel my load lighten. Thank You that You are gentle, and thank You for giving me rest for my weary soul. Amen.

THINK ABOUT IT:
What heavy burden will you offer to the Lord today?

Loving Fiercely

Ruth replied, "Don't urge me to leave you or to turn back from you. Where you go I will go, and where you stay I will stay. Your people will be my people and your God my God."
RUTH 1:16

Father, when I read the story of Ruth, a single woman who was far from the home where she was raised, I am impressed by her relationship with Naomi—the mother of the husband Ruth lost. And even though Naomi released her to return to her own family, Ruth was dogged in her commitment to Naomi and to You. I don't see that kind of tenacity much today, God, but I want to be a young woman who is *fierce* in my love for You and for others. Strengthen me to love fiercely today. Amen.

THINK ABOUT IT:
In which of your relationships, either divine or human, is God asking you to love doggedly?

....

....

....

....

....

....

....

....

....

What Makes Heaven Rejoice

I tell you that in the same way there will be more rejoicing in heaven over one sinner who repents than over ninety-nine righteous persons who do not need to repent.
LUKE 15:7

Lord, I confess that sometimes I take my salvation for granted. And yet when I listen to the stories that Jesus tells, I remember that there is great rejoicing when even one sinner repents. I believe that You delight in me, and I believe that Your heart longs to see others find You. God, let me be Your faithful witness today. Show me one person who needs to know about Your loving kindness, and equip me to share Your Gospel by my love, by my actions, and by my words. Amen.

THINK ABOUT IT:
Who in your life needs to know about the free grace God is offering them?

My Mind Is Set On You

You will keep in perfect peace those whose minds are steadfast, because they trust in you. Trust in the LORD forever, for the LORD, the LORD himself, is the Rock eternal.
ISAIAH 26:3–4

God, I turn to You today for help. My heart and mind and body are busy, and what I most need is Your peace. I read in Your Word that You give peace to those who trust in You, whose minds are steadfast. Lord, today I need Your help to fix my mind on You. Keep me from turning to shallow distractions, false substitutes that cannot satisfy my deepest desires. God, help me to keep my mind fixed steadfastly on You, my Rock Eternal. Amen.

THINK ABOUT IT:
What image, such as a rock, can you visualize when your busy mind gets distracted from trusting in God's faithfulness?

Bringing My Needs To God

"What do you want me to do for you?" Jesus asked him. The blind man said, "Rabbi, I want to see." "Go," said Jesus, "your faith has healed you." Immediately he received his sight and followed Jesus along the road.
MARK 10:51–52

Jesus, I believe You are the Great Physician who heals bodies and souls. Thank You, Lord. I confess, though, that sometimes I hesitate to ask You for what I most need. Instead I wrestle to manage on my own and do not ask for Your help. Forgive me, Lord. Today I am bold to bring my needs to You, confident that You listen and that You care. I ask for Your help, and I wait with patience and expectation to see what You will do. Amen.

THINK ABOUT IT:
What is a consistently pressing need in your life that you are slow to offer to God?

....

....

....

....

....

....

....

....

You Know Me Inside And Out

*My frame was not hidden from you when I was made
in the secret place, when I was woven together in the
depths of the earth. Your eyes saw my unformed body;
all the days ordained for me were written in your
book before one of them came to be.*
PSALM 139:15–16

Father, I thank You that You know me inside and out, and that You love me. Lord, I'm convinced that You know exactly what is happening in my life. You know the disappointment I felt yesterday. You know the challenge I'm battling today. And You know what I will face tomorrow. Nothing in my experience is hidden from You. None of it is a surprise. Lord, thank You that, in all things, You are with me and You are for me. Amen.

THINK ABOUT IT:
What would you prefer to keep hidden from God?

....

....

....

....

....

....

....

....

May Your Word Be Fulfilled

"I am the Lord's servant," Mary answered. "May your word to me be fulfilled." Then the angel left her.

LUKE 1:38

God, when I read the story of Your messenger visiting Mary, I am blown away! She was a teenager, like me. She was single, like me. And when You presented her with a pretty terrifying and life-altering plan, she said yes. God, it's hard for me to wrap my mind around the kind of trust she had in You. But in her heart, I see the kind of heart I desire. I want to be the girl who says, "Yes, I'm Yours. Do what You desire to do." I want a heart that is completely devoted to You and Your will. So today I welcome You to speak to me and use me for Your glory. Help me say yes! Amen.

THINK ABOUT IT:

When was the last time you heard God inviting you into something difficult, and you said yes?

No Escaping God's Reach

*If I take the wings of the morning and dwell in the
uttermost parts of the sea, even there your hand
shall lead me, and your right hand shall hold me.*
PSALM 139:9–10 ESV

Father, when I was a little girl, I thought I could hide from
the eyes of others. I fit in bedsheet play forts, big cardboard
boxes, and other secret hiding places. But You graciously
promise that there is nowhere I can go that is outside the
scope and reach of Your love. Even if I flee to the most re-
mote of places or am plunged into the depths of despair,
You hold me there. When I close my eyes, I can see myself
cradled in Your loving embrace. I thank You that You never
let me go. Amen.

THINK ABOUT IT:
*Where do you go, or what things do you do,
to try to escape from God?*

I Need Jesus

On hearing this, Jesus said, "It is not the healthy who need a doctor, but the sick. But go and learn what this means: 'I desire mercy, not sacrifice.' For I have not come to call the righteous, but sinners."
MATTHEW 9:12–13

Lord, when I go to school or church, I'm around people who give the impression that they don't even need You. On the outside, they look like they've got it all together. And so I try to act like that too. But when I'm honest with myself and with You, I know that I need You. And You confirm my suspicion when You say that You came for sinners. God, that's me! So I come to You, not as someone who's healthy and strong, but as someone who is sick and needs Your healing. Receive me, Lord, today. Amen.

THINK ABOUT IT:
*What broken or weak part of your life
most often draws you to Jesus?*

One Who Delights Over Me

"The LORD your God is with you, the Mighty Warrior who saves. He will take great delight in you; in his love he will no longer rebuke you, but will rejoice over you with singing."
ZEPHANIAH 3:17

God, I tip the eyes of my heart up toward heaven and I look for Your face. Sometimes when I search for You, I expect to see something that resembles the human faces I've known: a face that's distracted, or absent, or disappointed, or even angry. But that is not Your expression toward me. Instead, Your Word assures me that You *delight* in Your people! You even rejoice over us with singing! God, I have every confidence that today You are with me. Help me see You clearly so that I might receive Your great, great love. Amen.

THINK ABOUT IT:
*When you look toward God in prayer,
what expression do you see on His face?*

....

....

....

....

....

....

....

....

....

When I'm Down And When I'm Up

Is anyone among you in trouble? Let them pray. Is anyone happy? Let them sing songs of praise. Is anyone among you sick? Let them call the elders of the church to pray over them and anoint them with oil in the name of the Lord.
JAMES 5:13–14

Lord, You know how I am. When things are going great, I am happy to zip along without a nod of thanks to You. And when I'm struggling, when my life is in pieces, I'm the first person to bang on Your door. But I hear You calling me to something different, inviting me into *more*. Yes, You invite me, and others in Your body, to come to You when we're in trouble. Done! And You also invite us to turn to You when we're happy and when we're sick. God, quicken my heart and mind to bring everything in my day before You. Amen.

THINK ABOUT IT:
*What kinds of conversations do
you usually have with God?*

Known And Called

The word of the LORD came to me, saying, "Before I formed you in the womb I knew you, before you were born I set you apart; I appointed you as a prophet to the nations."
JEREMIAH 1:4–5

God, when I turn to Your Word, I see the way You called all kinds of unlikely people. You called a young boy named David, who became king, and a teenage girl named Mary, who gave birth to Jesus. You surprised everyone with Your unlikely choices! And even though Jeremiah thought he was too young and didn't have the right words, You called him to be Your prophet. God, I also believe You knew me and called me when I was still in my mother's womb. Help me pay attention today to the ways You want to use me to build Your kingdom. Amen.

THINK ABOUT IT:
As you've responded in obedience to God, have you ever had the sense, or awareness, that you were doing exactly what you were born to do?

....

....

....

....

....

....

....

Be Angry, Don't Sin

*"In your anger do not sin": Do not let the
sun go down while you are still angry,
and do not give the devil a foothold.*
EPHESIANS 4:26–27

God, there are days when I feel all the feels—including hot, fiery, explosive anger. I get upset with my family members. I get annoyed when I feel others have treated me unfairly. I even get furious at injustices that I see in the world. It's how You made me! And Your Word doesn't say that I *shouldn't* be angry. It says that when I am angry, I should not sin. God, help me be angry like that. Show me how to restore relationships damaged by outrage. Help me learn to make things right. And enable me to seek justice for the oppressed people You love. Let me use my anger for good, and help me to avoid sin. Amen.

THINK ABOUT IT:
*When did you sin against someone
else because you were angry?*

He Makes Me Lie Down

*The LORD is my shepherd, I lack nothing. He makes
me lie down in green pastures, he leads me
beside quiet waters, he refreshes my soul.*
PSALM 23:1–3

Although I know You invite me to rest, Lord, I find myself filling my time with all sorts of commitments and distractions. I give myself to school, to clubs, to sports, to activities, to service, to church, and to youth group. And then, if I have a free moment, I become absorbed in my phone, my laptop, or the television. God, I find it hard to be still. And yet I hear the gentle voice of my Shepherd inviting me to pause. To stop. To rest. God, You invite me to lie down in lush grass and stretch out beside quiet waters. Help me to pause. To stop. To rest. Amen.

THINK ABOUT IT:
*What is the best way for you to carve
out time to be still with God?*

Putting On The New Self

You were taught . . . to put off your old self, which is being corrupted by its deceitful desires; to be made new in the attitude of your minds; and to put on the new self, created to be like God in true righteousness and holiness.
EPHESIANS 4:22–24

God, I know that I am Yours and that I'm being transformed to look more like You. And in that process, I reflect the image of Christ. So I am taking off the old, dirty, ill-fitting clothes and behaviors that used to be mine. Cleaned up, I'm being transformed to look more like You. Lord, clothe me in Your righteousness and holiness, so that others can see You in me. Today I choose to discard the old and put on the new. Amen.

THINK ABOUT IT:
What about your old life, or deceitful desires, are you being invited to put behind you?

Putting A Friend Before Myself

After David had finished talking with Saul, Jonathan became one in spirit with David, and he loved him as himself. From that day Saul kept David with him and did not let him return home to his family. And Jonathan made a covenant with David because he loved him as himself.

1 SAMUEL 18:1–3

When I look at friendships in the Bible, God, one of the most beautiful is the relationship between David and Jonathan. When I read that Jonathan loved David "as himself," I know *exactly* what that means! I know how to make sure my needs are met, how to put myself before others, and even how to pursue getting what I want. And the kind of friendship between Jonathan and David is one in which the *other's* needs come first. Although this practice doesn't come naturally, teach me to love my friends like that. Amen.

THINK ABOUT IT:
When have you made a sacrifice for a friend?
When has a friend made a sacrifice for you?

Because God Loved Me, I Love

Dear friends, since God so loved us,
we also ought to love one another.
1 JOHN 4:11

Father in heaven, teach me to love like You do. I want to show Your love to those around me—my parents, my siblings, my friends, my classmates, and even strangers. But it can be hard! It's hard when others are being difficult. It's hard when I'm low on resources. It's hard when love requires sacrifice. And yet that costly kind of love is exactly what Jesus offered to the world—and offers to me. When I look at the life of Jesus—His words, His actions, His relationships—I know exactly what Your love is like. And because He loved me, I commit to offering others the same love. Amen.

THINK ABOUT IT:

How is the love that Jesus offers
different from ordinary human love?

Whatever, Whomever, Wherever, Whenever

The word of the LORD came to Jonah son of Amittai:
"Go to the great city of Nineveh and preach against it,
because its wickedness has come up before me."
JONAH 1:1–2

God, You know that I long to be Your faithful servant. And when You ask me to use my gifts to do things I enjoy—caring for children, serving elderly folks, or giving to those in need—I answer with a hearty *yes!* But there are other assignments—*You and I both know what they are*—that I am less enthusiastic about. When I'm honest, I'm a lot like Jonah. I may not want to go to that place, speak to that person, share that word, or give what I'd rather keep for myself. Forgive me and empower me to say yes to Your call—to do *whatever*, for *whomever*, *wherever*, and *whenever!* Amen.

THINK ABOUT IT:
When was the last time God asked
you to obey and you said no?

Speaking Only What Builds, Benefits, Blesses

Do not let any unwholesome talk come out of your mouths,
but only what is helpful for building others up according
to their needs, that it may benefit those who listen.
EPHESIANS 4:29

God, I want You to be the Lord of my tongue and the boss of whatever words come out of my mouth! I confess that it's tempting to use rough language because others think it's clever, funny, or edgy. It's tempting to talk about inappropriate subjects. And it's tempting to criticize, complain, or talk poorly about others. But Your Word is clear: I am to speak only words that build others up. God, that is a completely different vocabulary from the world's! Inspire and equip me to speak only words that will benefit others, to Your glory. Amen.

THINK ABOUT IT:
What areas of your speech do you
most need God's help to tame?

....

....

....

....

....

....

....

....

When I'm Low, He Lifts Me Up

*I waited patiently for the Lord; he turned to
me and heard my cry. He lifted me out of the
slimy pit, out of the mud and mire; he set my
feet on a rock and gave me a firm place to stand.*
Psalm 40:1–2

Lord, You know there are days when I am low—emotionally, spiritually, physically. There are days when I feel like I am sinking, stuck in a muddy pit, and I can't get out. But even in the pit, I know I'm not alone. You see me. You hear me. You help me. And, like the psalmist, sometimes I have to wait. And even though I want relief *right now*, I know that You are reliable, and You are with me. God, I'm counting on You to put my feet—my flip-flops, my sneakers, my boots, my heels—on solid ground. Amen.

THINK ABOUT IT:
*When was the last time you felt
low and the Lord helped you?*

Doing The Right Thing, The Right Way

Do everything without grumbling or arguing, so that you may become blameless and pure, "children of God without fault in a warped and crooked generation." Then you will shine among them like stars in the sky as you hold firmly to the word of life.
PHILIPPIANS 2:14–16

Lord, I thank You for calling me Your child. I want to live like I belong to You. Sometimes, even when I obey my parents or follow You, I do it with a grudging heart. I do the right thing but with the wrong attitude. But my aim is to be blameless before You. God, change my heart so that I can do all things to Your glory. I want to shine like a star in the sky for You. Amen.

THINK ABOUT IT:
What simple prayer can you breathe to God, asking Him for help when your heart is hard?

The Most Important Thing

Hear, O Israel: The LORD our God, the LORD is one. Love the LORD your God with all your heart and with all your soul and with all your strength. These commandments that I give you today are to be on your hearts.
DEUTERONOMY 6:4–6

God, as I navigate the waters of my life—at home, at school, and in the community—I need a rudder. And when I look to Your Word, I discover that You have given a clear directive that helps me steer through all I am facing. Your words in Deuteronomy tell me what Jesus later confirms: the most important thing is loving You with all my heart, all my soul, and all my strength. This is my rudder today. Amen.

THINK ABOUT IT:
How does your commitment to love God with all that you are impact the way you live this week?

....

....

....

....

....

....

....

....

....

Called God's Daughter

*You did not receive a spirit of slavery to fall back
into fear, but you have received a spirit of adoption.
When we cry, "Abba! Father!" it is that very Spirit bearing
witness with our spirit that we are children of God.*
ROMANS 8:15–16 NRSV

Father, because I am human, I see the ways that I am a slave
to sin. If I'm keeping it real, sometimes I enjoy wrongdoing
for a while, but it always becomes a cruel master. And yet
what is *most true* about me is that, through Jesus, You have
set me free from the power of sin and death by adopting me
as Your own daughter. And when I call you *Abba*, Father, my
spirit agrees with Your Spirit that I belong to You. Thank You
that Your love that sets me free is stronger than the slavery
of sin. Amen.

THINK ABOUT IT:
*How has God set you free
from the power of sin?*

You Hear My Cry

Hear my cry, O God; listen to my prayer. From the ends of the earth I call to you, I call as my heart grows faint; lead me to the rock that is higher than I. For you have been my refuge, a strong tower against the foe. I long to dwell in your tent forever and take refuge in the shelter of your wings.

PSALM 61:1–4

God, sometimes I feel like I am all alone. Even my family and friends don't seem to understand me completely. And so I turn to You. You have always been there for me when I've needed You in the past, and I trust that You are with me and for me today. God, when I'm with You, I feel safe and protected. I know, in my deepest places, that You hear my cry and listen to my prayer. And You care. Amen.

THINK ABOUT IT:
What do you want to share with God that you feel you can't share with anyone else?

Bearing Fruit

The fruit of the Spirit is love, joy, peace, forbearance,
kindness, goodness, faithfulness, gentleness and
self-control. Against such things there is no law.
Those who belong to Christ Jesus have crucified
the flesh with its passions and desires.
GALATIANS 5:22–24

Gracious God, I notice a tug inside me between what You've designed me for and what my flesh wants: pleasure, entertainment, distraction, satisfaction. Because I feel the pull and want to be faithful to You, I will water the seeds You have sown in my heart so that the fruit of Your Spirit might flourish in me. Let Your love, joy, peace, patience, kindness, goodness, faithfulness, gentleness, and self-control live in me and through me. May others who see my life taste and see that *You are good!* Amen.

THINK ABOUT IT:
Among the fruit of the Spirit, which is the most challenging
for you to produce, causing you to depend on God's help?

Hearing And Doing

Do not merely listen to the word,
and so deceive yourselves. Do what it says.
JAMES 1:22

Father God, I thank You that I am Yours. I have Your Word. I am part of a body of believers, and I am grateful for my peers and those adults who can help me grow. But it can be easy to coast: to show up at church, to listen to Christian music, even to flip open my Bible and say some prayers. But I don't want to be someone who grows fat on Your Word. I want to be the girl who hears Your Word and does what it says. God, strengthen me this week to love my neighbor, to care for those on the world's margins, to share Your good news with others, and to glorify You in all I do. I commit myself to being not just a faithful listener but a faithful follower. Amen.

THINK ABOUT IT:
How is God inviting you to put His Word
into practice in your life this week?

Honoring My Parents

*Children, obey your parents in the Lord, for this is right.
"Honor your father and mother"—which is the first
commandment with a promise—"so that it may go well
with you and that you may enjoy long life on the earth."*
EPHESIANS 6:1–3

Father, I have heard Your instruction to honor my parents—
both in the Old Testament's Ten Commandments and in
Paul's letter to the church in Ephesus. I hear You, Lord.
Your Word clearly says that I am to respect, love, and honor
my parents. Sometimes that's really easy, but sometimes I
struggle to obey Your Word. God, be my Helper as I purpose
to honor my parents—with my attitude, with my words, and
with my actions—so that You may be glorified. Amen.

THINK ABOUT IT:
*When do you find it most difficult to obey
God's command to honor your parents?*

Here I Am, Lord

The LORD called Samuel. Samuel answered,
"Here I am." And he ran to Eli and said, "Here I am;
you called me." But Eli said, "I did not call; go back
and lie down." So he went and lay down.
1 SAMUEL 3:4–5

God, I thank You that You chose to call Samuel, who was just a boy, to serve You. Just as You called Samuel, I believe You still call Your people—Your *young* people!—to know You and to serve You. Lord, I am listening for Your voice. Even if it's not audible to others, I believe that You speak to my heart. God, teach me how to serve You today. Like Samuel, I am eager and ready to respond by serving You with joy and faithfulness. Speak, Lord. Amen.

THINK ABOUT IT:
What is something God has been calling you
to do that you need to say yes to, today?

Loving Like Jesus Loved

We love because he first loved us.
1 JOHN 4:19

Jesus, You know what this world is like. People are divided socially, economically, politically, ethnically, and even spiritually. The world insists that I should love those who look like I look, speak as I speak, live where I live, behave the way I behave, and worship where I worship. The world even gives me permission to ignore those who are different from me. And yet when I look at You, I see a radically different way of being in the world. I see Someone who chose to love those who were the "wrong" race, "wrong" gender, "wrong" religion. You didn't just receive those who were different from You, You pursued them in love. You pursued *me* in love. Because You loved me first, teach me to love others with that same love. Amen.

THINK ABOUT IT:
*Who is it that God is inviting you to know
and love who is different from you?*

....

....

....

....

....

....

....

....

My Body Is Good

You created my inmost being; you knit me together
in my mother's womb. I praise you because I am
fearfully and wonderfully made; your works
are wonderful, I know that full well.
PSALM 139:13–14

Creator God, You lovingly created the world, and I believe
that includes *me*! I was not an accident. When I was in my
mother's womb, You knit me together: my hair, my skin, my
eyes, my nose, my frame. You saw Your handiwork, and You
called it *good*. You call *me* good. Because You are my Maker,
I ignore the voices swirling around me that insist I'm too
tall or too short, too light or too dark, too fat or too thin.
Instead I turn my eyes toward Your smiling face. I bend my
ear toward Your voice, which confirms that I am fearfully
and wonderfully made. I trust in what You say about me
today. Amen.

THINK ABOUT IT:
Where do you hear messages that lie
about the value of your body?

Convinced That God Is For Me

What, then, shall we say in response to these things?
If God is for us, who can be against us?
ROMANS 8:31

Faithful God, it is obvious that what we experience in this world is often not Your will. Children go hungry. They get sick. They endure abuse. Adults argue. They lose their jobs. They leave their homes and families. Communities fail to care for those in need, and nations wage war. God, I don't know how to make sense of such suffering. But in the midst of the chaos, whether in my life or in the world, I am certain of one thing: You are *for* me. No matter what I face, I have the confidence that You see, You care, and *You are for me.* Amen.

THINK ABOUT IT:

In what situation in your life this week do you most need to hang on to the truth that God is with you and for you?

What Matters Most

Charm is deceptive, and beauty is fleeting;
but a woman who fears the LORD is to be praised.
PROVERBS 31:30

God of love, it is no secret what the world prizes today: bodies that are model-fit, faces that are camera-ready, fashions that change with every season. The people who get the most attention are those with plenty of followers, clever posts, and lots of likes. Honestly, trying to be such a person is *exhausting*. And that's why I'm so grateful to find rest in You, because You don't ask for any of that. Instead of seeking the praise of others, I am interested in Your opinion only. I'm grateful that all You ask is that I fear You, know You, love You. And I do. Today I'll walk in the freedom of Your love. Amen.

THINK ABOUT IT:
What could be different in your life if you let go
of your efforts to squeeze into the world's mold
and rested in God's approval instead?

....

....

....

....

....

....

....

Hope In The Healer

A woman who had suffered from a discharge of blood for twelve years came up behind him and touched the fringe of his garment, for she said to herself, "If I only touch his garment, I will be made well." Jesus turned, and seeing her he said, "Take heart, daughter; your faith has made you well."
MATTHEW 9:20–22 ESV

Lord, I can't imagine what it would be like to bleed for twelve years. This woman You touched, who'd been ostracized by her community for being "unclean," must have been so weak physically, emotionally, and spiritually. She had hope in You, and You healed her. Lord, give me faith like this woman's. I offer You my tender broken places with the confidence that You care for me. Amen.

THINK ABOUT IT:
*Is there something in your heart or body
in need of Jesus' healing touch today?*

Speaking Up

If you remain silent at this time, relief and deliverance for the Jews will arise from another place, but you and your father's family will perish. And who knows but that you have come to your royal position for such a time as this?
ESTHER 4:14

When You chose Esther, Lord, you picked someone wildly unlikely to influence her culture. She was the wrong gender, wrong race, wrong religion. And yet when You gave her a big assignment, to speak truth to power, she said *yes*. She was brave. She was bold. She was faithful to You. God, I believe that You call unlikely young women today to speak bravely and boldly about what is wrong in our world. Give me Your courage to be faithful to You by telling the truth in love. Amen.

THINK ABOUT IT:
What problem in your school, community, or world is God inviting you to address?

....

....

....

....

....

....

....

....

Serving My Friends Like Jesus Served His

*He poured water into a basin and began
to wash his disciples' feet, drying them with
the towel that was wrapped around him.*
JOHN 13:5

Faithful God, when You came to us in the person of Jesus, You turned everything upside down. Instead of coming to be served, You came to serve. That was countercultural back then, and it is still radical today! Lord, in John's Gospel I see what that kind of love looks like. I can see You kneeling on the ground, wiping the feet of Your friends. Teach me to love people like that. Today I commit to serving others— my friends, my parents, my siblings, and others—without demanding anything in return. Empower me to show others what Your love is like. Amen.

THINK ABOUT IT:
*How can you love others around
you with the humility of Jesus?*

When I'm Low, The Lord Is Near

The LORD is close to the brokenhearted
and saves those who are crushed in spirit.
PSALM 34:18

God, I thank You that You know me inside and out. You know the days when I'm flying high, full of joy and life. And You know the days when I struggle to keep it together. On those days when it's hard to get out of bed, when I'm feeling crushed, I trust that You are with me. When it feels like no one else gets it, Your Word promises me that You are ready to help. God, open my eyes today to see Your face shining upon me. Thank You for being near and for holding me in Your care when I feel so alone. Amen.

THINK ABOUT IT:
On your hardest days, can you close your eyes
and picture God's gracious face looking upon you?

Giving Back To God

Remember this: Whoever sows sparingly will also reap sparingly, and whoever sows generously will also reap generously. Each of you should give what you have decided in your heart to give, not reluctantly or under compulsion, for God loves a cheerful giver.
2 CORINTHIANS 9:6–7

God, when I hear Your call to give, I want to believe that it is for other people. But I know that You are inviting *me* to give joyfully to You, for the work of Your kingdom. I don't have a lot of money, but I offer You a portion of what You've given me. Show me how You would have me use that faithfully. And I also offer You my time and energy. Show me how You're calling me to use the particular gifts You've given me to build Your kingdom. All I have belongs to You. Amen.

THINK ABOUT IT:
If you're not currently giving to God from your money, what financial commitment might God be inviting you to make?

The One Thing You Treasure

His pleasure is not in the strength of the horse, nor his delight in the legs of the warrior; the LORD delights in those who fear him, who put their hope in his unfailing love.
PSALM 147:10–11

Lord, when I spend time in Your Word, I am reminded that Your priorities turn the world's values upside down. When Jesus ushered in the new kingdom, He announced through His words and His actions that the first would be last and the last would be first. Here in the Psalms, I read that You value people so differently from the way the world values people. While we value power, strength, and beauty, You delight in one thing: those who put their trust in Your unfailing love. God, help me to be single-minded as I purpose to trust You in all things. Amen.

THINK ABOUT IT:
Is there a situation in your life right now that you can't manage? What would it look like to entrust those circumstances to God?

Forgiving As I've Been Forgiven

Bear with each other and forgive one another
if any of you has a grievance against someone.
Forgive as the Lord forgave you.
COLOSSIANS 3:13

God, I thank You that, in Jesus, You gave Your life so that my sins might be forgiven. You redeemed me once and for all when I came to know You, and You continue to forgive my sins day by day. I am grateful for Your abundant mercy. At the same time, I struggle to be as merciful to others as You have been to me! I harbor hurts from family members, I nurse wounds from friends, and I hold on to slights from others. But You invite me into a better way, challenging me to forgive others the same way You forgive me—which is mercifully and generously! Lord, strengthen me to be quick to forgive others. Amen.

THINK ABOUT IT:
Is there a person in your life today whom God
is asking you to forgive once and for all?

Resisting The Devil, Drawing Near To God

Submit yourselves, then, to God. Resist the devil, and he will flee from you. Come near to God and he will come near to you. Wash your hands, you sinners, and purify your hearts, you double-minded.
JAMES 4:7–8

Even though I can't see it with my eyes, Lord, I feel the tug between good and evil in my life. And even though I know and love You, I'm tempted to do the things I don't want to do, and I'm slow to obey You. But Your Word reminds me that I'm not a helpless victim in a heavenly battle. This week, empower me to resist the devil, saying a strong *no* to temptation. And resisting the devil, God, I draw near to You. As I fall into Your loving arms, I feel Your secure embrace. I submit myself to You and trust in Your mercy. Amen.

THINK ABOUT IT:
In what specific way can you make a choice to resist evil this week?

Offering My Hurts To God

Do not say, "I'll pay you back for this wrong!"
Wait for the LORD, and he will avenge you.
PROVERBS 20:22

Faithful God, thank You that I can trust You with the most tender matters of the heart. You know the ways that I have been bumped, bruised, and battered throughout my life. And You know the hearts of those who've wronged me. I admit that it's tempting to want to respond in anger, to speak unkind words, and to even the score by returning wrong for wrong. But I hear Your voice of wisdom calming my heart, inviting me to trust You. God, I offer You the hurts I've received from others. I release them into Your keeping so I don't have to carry them anymore. Thank You for Your mercy and Your care for me. Amen.

THINK ABOUT IT:
Is there a wrong you've suffered that
you need to release to God today?

Given A New Heart

"I will give you a new heart, and a new spirit I will put within you. And I will remove the heart of stone from your flesh and give you a heart of flesh."
EZEKIEL 36:26 ESV

Lord, You promise that You are removing my heart of stone and giving me a new heart and a new spirit. This is what I need! My heart is hard because I've chosen to disobey what I know is right. My heart is hard from the times I've ignored Your voice. And my heart is also hard from the defenses I've put up to protect myself from getting hurt by others. Because I believe that You can be trusted with my heart, I offer it to You, the Good Physician, and I welcome the new heart You are knitting together inside me. Amen.

THINK ABOUT IT:
What do you see in the hardened heart you are releasing into God's care?

A Face That Is Kind

Many of the Samaritans from that town believed in him
because of the woman's testimony, "He told me everything
I ever did." So when the Samaritans came to him, they
urged him to stay with them, and he stayed two days. And
because of his words many more became believers.
JOHN 4:39–41

Lord, I am blown away when I listen in on the conversation between Jesus and a woman who was known in her town as a dirty, despised, no-good sinner. From my human perspective, I would expect her heart to harden against Him the way mine would if someone was up in my business! And yet her exuberant testimony reveals what words cannot: she felt received and loved by Jesus, and her witness convinces me that He treated her kindly and graciously. Lord, open my eyes to see Your mercy toward me as well. Amen.

THINK ABOUT IT:
When you close your eyes, can you see the
kind, gracious, merciful face of Jesus?

....

....

....

....

....

....

....

Fleeing From Danger

The prudent see danger and take refuge,
but the simple keep going and pay the penalty.
PROVERBS 22:3

God, open my heart to hear, receive, and put into practice the rich wisdom I'm finding in Your Word. Help me learn and grow from Your ancient teachings about how to live well. I'm thinking especially about situations in my life that could pose danger: lying to my parents, cheating at school, driving with people who've been drinking, trying drugs, and saying *yes* to other unwise risks. Your Word convinces me that not only do I need to say *no*, I need to shelter myself from these temptations, even when it's not popular. Lord, give me the courage to recognize dangerous choices and take refuge in You. Amen.

THINK ABOUT IT:
What situation or temptation are you
facing that could be dangerous?

....

....

....

....

....

....

....

....

Giving God My Gifts

He and all his companions were astonished at the catch of fish they had taken, and so were James and John, the sons of Zebedee, Simon's partners. Then Jesus said to Simon, "Don't be afraid; from now on you will fish for people." So they pulled their boats up on shore, left everything and followed him.

LUKE 5:9–11

When I witness the way Jesus engaged and called a band of fishermen at the seashore, I notice a restlessness in my own heart to follow You. You took what these men had—the ability to fish—and redeemed it for the good of Your kingdom. Lord, today I offer You my own gifts—my creativity, my physical strength, my intellect, my generosity, my problem-solving skills, everything You've given me—and I ask You to use me. Speak, Lord, Your servant is listening. Amen.

THINK ABOUT IT:
What is one particular gift, skill, or passion God has given you that can be used to build His kingdom?

....

....

....

....

....

....

....

God Of Power And Surprise

When Pharaoh's horses, chariots and horsemen went into the sea, the LORD brought the waters of the sea back over them, but the Israelites walked through the sea on dry ground.
EXODUS 15:19

When Your people who were oppressed as slaves in Egypt cried out to You, You heard their pleas. And when You called them out of bondage, Lord, You went *big*. When they fled—without weapons, without protection, without provision—You defended them and toppled the warriors who pursued them. In a mighty act of power that no one saw coming, You rescued Your people. God, I'm convinced that You are the same all-merciful, all-powerful Savior today. I see how You make a way where it seems there isn't one, and so I'm willing to trust You with the big stuff in my life because You can do all things. Amen.

THINK ABOUT IT:
*Where are you stuck or suffering right now,
a place that you can't manage on your own?*

Avoiding The Drama

Have nothing to do with foolish, ignorant controversies;
you know that they breed quarrels. And the Lord's
servant must not be quarrelsome but kind to everyone,
able to teach, patiently enduring evil, correcting his
opponents with gentleness. God may perhaps grant
them repentance leading to a knowledge of the truth.
2 TIMOTHY 2:23–25 ESV

Lord, You know the foolishness that gets stirred up among people: this comment on social media, that social slight, this accusation, or that gossip. And it's so easy to get sucked into the drama! Father, I want to live differently, as one who shines Your light in the world—at home, at school, at church, and in the world. Help me exercise wisdom and avoid useless controversies. I trust You to be my Helper as I show others Your kindness. Amen.

THINK ABOUT IT:
How will you choose to avoid conflicts
that only tear others down?

I Fear No Evil

*Even though I walk through the darkest valley,
I will fear no evil, for you are with me; your
rod and your staff, they comfort me.*
PSALM 23:4

God, I confess that when I'm stumbling through my own dark nights—when I'm hurt, when I'm lost, when I'm blinded, when I can't see what's ahead—I feel afraid. And yet You promise that in the darkest of valleys, You are with me. I can have confidence that I don't need to be afraid because You're near. You guide me, even though I can't see. You lead me, even when I'm limping. Lord, teach me to trust in Your nearness. Amen.

THINK ABOUT IT:
*When was the last time you felt overwhelmed
by darkness and needed to trust in God?*

What Matters Most

Set your minds on things above, not on earthly things.
For you died, and your life is now hidden with Christ in God.
COLOSSIANS 3:2–3

Father, You know how full my heart and mind are. So often I'm busy thinking about things of the flesh: my hurting feet, my next snack, the cute boy in my second period class, the outfit I want to buy at the mall, the number of calories in a cup of juice, or the newest lyrics from my favorite recording artist. And although none of those thoughts are bad, they can distract me from what matters most. So be my Helper today so I can set my mind on the things that matter most to You. Wrap me in Your warm embrace, because my life is now hidden with Christ in You. Amen.

THINK ABOUT IT:

When you find your mind bouncing from
distraction to distraction, what one scripture
or thought can help you refocus?

A New Mind

Be changed within by a new way of thinking. Then you will be able to decide what God wants for you; you will know what is good and pleasing to him and what is perfect.
ROMANS 12:2 NCV

God who created my mind and all that I am, I offer myself to You. Daily my thoughts are influenced by the world's loud messages that I see and hear in advertisements, television shows, songs, movies, and even in what my friends post on social media. But I thank You that You're at work renewing my mind to embrace a new way of thinking. And thank You for the confidence that, by Your Spirit, I can know what is good. I can know what pleases You. I can know what is perfect. Lord, guide my thoughts and decisions today. Amen.

THINK ABOUT IT:
What are the ways God is transforming your mind?

....

....

....

....

....

....

....

....

....

Thrown Into The Depths Of The Sea

Who is a God like you, who pardons sin and forgives the transgression of the remnant of his inheritance? You do not stay angry forever but delight to show mercy. You will again have compassion on us; you will tread our sins underfoot and hurl all our iniquities into the depths of the sea.
MICAH 7:18–19

Lord, when I confess my sins to You, I don't always let go of them. Your Word promises me that You have compassion on me and forgive me. But I am tempted to hang on to my sins. To remember them. And even to feel guilty about things you have forgiven. God, today I choose to trust in the promise of Your Word. Not only have You have hurled my sins into the depths of the sea, but You delight in showing mercy. Change my heart to match Yours! Amen.

THINK ABOUT IT:
Is there a particular sin, or pattern of sin, that you need to release completely to God?

....
....
....
....
....
....
....
....

Setting An Example For Others

Command and teach these things. Don't let anyone look down on you because you are young, but set an example for the believers in speech, in conduct, in love, in faith and in purity.
1 Timothy 4:11–12

God, I notice how people look at me because I'm a teen. They assume I'm shallow, or immature, or foolish, or without faith in You. But I'm convinced that You've called me to be a follower of Jesus and a leader of people. And so I take my marching orders from You. Guide me as I purpose to set an example for other Christians with my life. I long to honor You with the words of my mouth, with my behavior, with my love for others, with my faith in You, and with my pure heart. Help me to show the world who You are and who You've made me to be. Amen.

THINK ABOUT IT:
What is one way to show others that you belong to God and are guided by Him?

Uniquely Gifted

If the whole body were an eye, where would be the sense of hearing? If the whole body were an ear, where would be the sense of smell? But as it is, God arranged the members in the body, each one of them, as he chose.
1 Corinthians 12:17–18 esv

Father, sometimes when I look at the gifts others have, I feel jealous. I notice the creativity that she has. Or the writing gifts he has. Or the athletic skill she has. But I trust that You have given gifts exactly as You have chosen. And I am confident that You have equipped me with all I need to serve as a member of Your body. Lord, I commit all that I have and all that I am to You and to Your kingdom. Amen.

THINK ABOUT IT:
What are some of the talents, gifts, skills, abilities, and passions God has given you? And how can they be used to build His kingdom?

Being Good In Secret

"Be especially careful when you are trying to be good so that you don't make a performance out of it. It might be good theater, but the God who made you won't be applauding."
MATTHEW 6:1 MSG

You know my heart, Lord. You know that I long to live a life that is pleasing to You. And You also know that I struggle against the natural human temptation to let others know what I'm up to: to be sure they see me bowing my head before a meal, to mention the child I sponsor overseas, or to point out the ways I've served in my community. You know that's not who I want to be. So I commit to keeping quiet about the good I do, to keeping it just between You and me. Our secret! Cleanse my heart so that I might love and serve You well. Amen.

THINK ABOUT IT:
*Is there a way in which you're tempted
to make your good works public?*

....

....

....

....

....

....

....

....

Trusting God In The Present Moment

Do not worry about tomorrow, for tomorrow will worry about itself. Each day has enough trouble of its own.
MATTHEW 6:34

God, I trust You with all of my yesterdays, I trust You with today, and I trust You with all my tomorrows. I confess that when I start to think about what comes next—making the team, finding a part-time job, getting into college, figuring out how my family will *pay* for college, deciding what I'll do when I grow up—my mind can get away from me. And yet when I turn my eyes toward You, I feel my heart settle down. And I hear You calling me to stay in the present moment and pay attention to what's in front of me. Help me, because I trust in You. Amen.

THINK ABOUT IT:

What worries you the most when you think about the future?

....

....

....

....

....

....

....

....

Words That Are Sweet And Healing

Gracious words are a honeycomb,
sweet to the soul and healing to the bones.
PROVERBS 16:24

God, Your Word says that the tongue is powerful. And my experience has proven that to be true. Others' unkind or untrue words have cut me and made me feel small. But their generous ones have strengthened me, nourished me, and built me up. God, as I listen to the words that are spoken by my friends, my classmates, my teachers, my parents, my mentors, and others, I'm reminded that I want to be one of those people who uses my words for *good*. I want the words I speak to others to be "sweet to the soul and healing to the bones." Send Your Spirit to guide my tongue, so that I might bless those around me by using gracious speech. Amen.

THINK ABOUT IT:
Who is one person you know who builds
others up by the way he or she speaks?

....

....

....

....

....

....

....

....

Giving My Thoughts To God

Whatsoever things are true, whatsoever things are honest, whatsoever things are just, whatsoever things are pure, whatsoever things are lovely, whatsoever things are of good report; if there be any virtue, and if there be any praise, think on these things.
PHILIPPIANS 4:8 KJV

Lord, I confess that I am tempted to think about things that don't help me grow to be more like Jesus. Whether it's the music I put in my ears, the shows and movies I watch with my eyes, or even the ways that my imagination can get away from me, I know I need Your help. This week, when I notice thoughts that don't honor You, help me replace them with all that is true, honest, just, pure, lovely, and good. Thank You for being my Helper. Amen.

THINK ABOUT IT:
Can you think of one true and pure thought that can serve as a "replacement" for the thoughts in your head that are less helpful?

God Revives My Heart

Create in me a pure heart, O God, and renew a steadfast spirit within me. Do not cast me from your presence or take your Holy Spirit from me. Restore to me the joy of your salvation and grant me a willing spirit, to sustain me.
PSALM 51:10–12

God, I thank You that You know my heart. You know when I'm soaring high: after receiving good news, or doing great on a test, or winning an award, or surprising a friend. And You know when my heart is low: when my emotions are low, or when I've been disappointed, or when I've sinned. You know my heart, and You promise to renew and revive it. God, allow Your Spirit to move within me so my heart may be pure and I may rejoice in You. Amen.

THINK ABOUT IT:
Is there something you're holding in your heart—a sadness, a sin—that you want to release to God's Spirit today?

Sharing The Love

*As God's chosen people, holy and dearly
loved, clothe yourselves with compassion,
kindness, humility, gentleness and patience.*
COLOSSIANS 3:12

God, You know the kinds of qualities that are prized among my generation: sarcasm, smart comebacks, clever tear-downs, and just plan meanness. And yet, as Your daughter, I'm convinced that You have called me to operate differently. Be my Helper as I purpose to represent You in my life today. Where there is coolness, let me offer compassion. When others are mean, let me share kindness. Where there is pride, let me practice humility. When others are harsh, teach me to be gentle. And when others are hurried, let me exercise patience. God, fill me with Your Spirit so that I might live as Your holy and dearly loved child. Amen.

THINK ABOUT IT:

*As one who is dearly loved, how is God calling you
to treat others as those who are also dearly loved?*

....

....

....

....

....

....

....

God Protects Me From Evil

*My prayer is not that you take them out of the world
but that you protect them from the evil one.*
JOHN 17:15

Father God, I am blessed when I eavesdrop on the very prayers that Jesus prayed for His followers—that Jesus prayed for me! And I hear that He didn't pray that my life would be easy. Or that I would be rich. Or that I'd never struggle. Or that I'd never fail. Jesus prayed that *You would protect me* from the evil one. God, that is my prayer today as well. By Your grace, I reject the lies of my adversary. Help me to recognize his wily schemes, and strengthen me by the power of Your Word and Your Spirit. I am confident that You are my good Protector, in Jesus' name. Amen.

THINK ABOUT IT:
*Where do you most clearly see the
work of the evil one in the world?*

....

....

....

....

....

....

....

....

Staying Humble

Pride goes before destruction,
a haughty spirit before a fall.
PROVERBS 16:18

You warn us, God, that pride goes before a fall. And I confess that I want to believe that is true of others, but not of me. And yet this wisdom resonates as being true for me too! God, I long for my heart to be humble before You. When I succeed in school, let me be humble. When I succeed in athletics, let me be humble. When I am thriving socially, let me be humble. When I receive awards, let me be humble. And even when I am granted spiritual favor from You, let me be humble. May my posture of confident humility communicate to others that You are the Source of all good things in my life. Amen.

THINK ABOUT IT:

Is there an area in your life in which
it is most difficult to remain humble?

Helping My Friends Meet Jesus

Since they could not get him to Jesus because of the crowd, they made an opening in the roof above Jesus by digging through it and then lowered the mat the man was lying on. When Jesus saw their faith, he said to the paralyzed man, "Son, your sins are forgiven."
MARK 2:4–5

Thank You, Father, for the stories of Jesus in the Gospels that reveal His character, and Yours. And thank You, in particular, that Mark recounted this story of four men who believed that Jesus could heal their friend, in body and soul. Their dogged faithfulness reminds me that I'm also called to carry my friends to Jesus. Quicken my heart and mind to find creative ways to introduce my friends to Jesus, so that He can meet their deep needs. Amen.

THINK ABOUT IT:
Has God already put a particular friend, someone who needs to know the transforming power of Jesus, on your heart?

....

....

....

....

....

....

....

....

Choosing Contentment

I have learned in whatever situation I am to be content.
I know how to be brought low, and I know how to abound.
In any and every circumstance, I have learned the secret
of facing plenty and hunger, abundance and need. I can
do all things through him who strengthens me.
PHILIPPIANS 4:11–13 ESV

Father, the culture around me insists that I deserve more food, more fashion, more entertainment, more pleasure. But when I agree, when I scramble after more and more, I always end up feeling empty. You offer another way. And when I choose contentment, when I choose gratitude, when I choose to joyfully receive what You have given, then I am finally *full*. Teach me to choose contentment in every situation, for Your glory and for my good. Amen.

THINK ABOUT IT:
For what can you give God
thanks and praise today?

Signs Of My Heart Health

You brood of vipers, how can you who are evil say anything good? For the mouth speaks what the heart is full of.
MATTHEW 12:34

Lord Jesus, although You were rebuking Pharisees whose hearts were hardened toward You, I also hear Your voice speaking to me. What comes out of *my* mouth reveals what is in my heart. And I invite You to help me notice and deal with what I find there. When my language reveals fear and anxiety, help me discern what is troubling my heart. When my speech is negative, critical, or unkind, help me discern what is brewing in my heart. When my words are sad and without hope, help me discern what is simmering in my heart. When I explode with anger or rage, help me discern what is boiling in my heart. God, reveal what is in my heart and heal my inner being. Amen.

THINK ABOUT IT:
*What sorts of signals do your words
reveal about what's in your heart?*

....

....

....

....

....

....

....

....

Hungering For What God Provides

*Jesus, full of the Holy Spirit, left the Jordan and was led
by the Spirit into the wilderness, where for forty days he
was tempted by the devil. He ate nothing during those
days, and at the end of them he was hungry.*
LUKE 4:1–2

Jesus, when You chose to come to earth as a man, You encountered the same temptations I do. And yet the *way* You dealt with them is so different from the ways I do. When I face trials, I scramble to make sure my needs are met, comforting myself with food, shopping, other people, entertainment, and more. But when I look to Your example, I see that when You faced trials, You *fasted*! Rather than meeting Your own needs, You chose instead to radically trust in Your Father's provision. When You were weakest, You were strongest. Help me to choose this holy way. Amen.

THINK ABOUT IT:
*What are the ways you're tempted to soothe
yourself when you're facing trials or temptations?*

God Sees. Hears. Knows. Cares

*The Israelites groaned in their slavery and cried out,
and their cry for help because of their slavery went up to
God. God heard their groaning and he remembered his
covenant with Abraham, with Isaac and with Jacob. So God
looked on the Israelites and was concerned about them.*
EXODUS 2:23–25

God, when Your people were suffering in Egypt, You did not abandon them. And Your faithfulness to them tells me so much about Your faithfulness to me: You noticed their suffering; You heard their cries; You remembered Your covenant; You cared for them. God, I thank You that, because You do not change, You see, You hear, You know, and You care when I am hurting too. God, like Your people in Egypt, I lift up my voice to You with all my needs, confident in Your mercy and power. Amen.

THINK ABOUT IT:
*What suffering in your life is God
inviting you to share with Him?*

Loving Those Who Don't Love Me

*If you love those who love you, what reward will you get?
Are not even the tax collectors doing that? And if you
greet only your own people, what are you doing more
than others? Do not even pagans do that?*
MATTHEW 5:46–47

God, You know how people naturally operate, and You know how I operate. It's easy for me to love those who love me: my family, my friends, my pastors, my teachers. (That's what everyone does, even people who don't know You!) But You have called me to a higher standard of love. So open my eyes to the folks who are harder to love. The ones who are different from me. Even the ones who might be rude or mean. Show me how to love them the way You do, so that they might discover Your love and goodness. Be my Helper, in Jesus' name. Amen.

THINK ABOUT IT:
*Who is God inviting you to care for,
even if that person doesn't yet love you?*

Giver Of All Good Gifts

*Every good and perfect gift is from above, coming
down from the Father of the heavenly lights,
who does not change like shifting shadows.*
JAMES 1:17

God, I thank You that You are a good Provider, and I acknowledge that all good gifts come from You. I confess that I don't always thank You for Your generosity toward me. Too often I assume that I *deserve* the privileges I enjoy. Or I believe that what I have is because I worked hard or my parents worked hard. I might even just fail to notice and be grateful for all that I enjoy. So today I pause to thank You for the home in which I live, the clothes that are on my back, the food that is on my table, and the people who love me. You have provided so abundantly for me! Thank You. Amen.

THINK ABOUT IT:
*What are the ways you have been
noticing God's provision in your life?*

Meditating On God's Word

Blessed is the one who does not walk in step with the wicked or stand in the way that sinners take or sit in the company of mockers, but whose delight is in the law of the Lord, and who meditates on his law day and night.

PSALM 1:1–2

Lord, thank You for the richness of Your holy Word, which I can chew on day and night. In the ancient stories of Your people, I discover Your character. In writings like the Psalms, I listen in on the prayers of Your people. In the books of the prophets, I discover Your holy passion for justice. In the Gospels, I see You clearly in the person of Jesus. I glimpse the witness of Your earliest followers. I listen in on letters sent among the earliest churches. And I savor the vision of what is to come in Your kingdom. Today I gratefully hold the riches of Your Word in my heart. Amen.

THINK ABOUT IT:
What portion of God's Word are you holding in your heart today?

Known And Remembered By God

The LORD answers, "Can a woman forget the baby she nurses? Can she feel no kindness for the child to which she gave birth? Even if she could forget her children, I will not forget you. See, I have written your name on my hand."
ISAIAH 49:15–16 NCV

Lord, the voice that lies tries to convince me that my life is not precious to others and is not precious to You. The deceiver says that the human mother and father who bore me do not love me. That friends don't care for me. That others overlook me. But You? You assure me that my name is written on Your hand. That You hold me. That You notice me and love me. Today I trust the promise I have in Your Word. Amen.

THINK ABOUT IT:
Can you close your eyes and see your name tattooed on God's hand?

The Word That Is Active And Alive

*The word of God is alive and active. Sharper
than any double-edged sword, it penetrates even
to dividing soul and spirit, joints and marrow;
it judges the thoughts and attitudes of the heart.*
HEBREWS 4:12

Lord, I give You thanks and praise for Your Word. And I believe that in the Old and New Testaments, I find the words of life. Although the lying voice of the enemy whispers that Your Word is antiquated and outdated, I know better. Your Word is not dead; it's alive! And in its pages I can see Your faithfulness to Your people throughout the ages. I discover Your character. I witness Your love. And I am strengthened and guided in living the rich, full life that You've given me. Amen.

THINK ABOUT IT:
*What scripture passage is God inviting you to study today?
Where are you camped out in God's Word?*

Giving My Life For Others

*"I am the good shepherd. The good
shepherd lays down his life for the sheep."*
JOHN 10:11

God, throughout the ages You have made Yourself known to
Your people as the Good Shepherd. The writer of Psalm 23
encountered You in this way, and in the person of Jesus I see
exactly what Your gracious shepherding love is like. Thank
You. In Jesus' sacrifice, and even in His daily living, I see the
ways He gave His life for me and for others. Teach me to
love like Jesus loved, giving up what I want for the good of
other people. As I seek to pattern my life after Jesus, show
me how to care for my friends, my family, and the world by
imitating Jesus' sacrificial love. Amen.

THINK ABOUT IT:

*As you think about those whom God has
called you to love, is there a way you're
being invited to sacrifice on their behalf?*

The One Who Does Not Slumber

He will not let your foot slip—he who watches over you will not slumber; indeed, he who watches over Israel will neither slumber nor sleep. The LORD watches over you— the LORD is your shade at your right hand; the sun will not harm you by day, nor the moon by night.
PSALM 121:3–6

God, when I lay down in my bed at night, You know that my mind keeps whirring. I think about all the things I need to get done. I brood on things that aren't fruitful. I worry about stuff I can't control. I resist sleep because, in my mind, I am busy managing the world! But Your Word reminds me that I can let go because You are God. While I slumber, You remain wakeful to Your world and to me. You watch over me as my Good Protector. Thank You, Father. Amen.

THINK ABOUT IT:
What is one concern you cling to that God is inviting you to release into His care?

The Most Important Thing

"The most important one," answered Jesus, "is this: 'Hear, O Israel: The Lord our God, the Lord is one. Love the Lord your God with all your heart and with all your soul and with all your mind and with all your strength.'"
MARK 12:29–30

Lord Jesus, every day I have to make choices about how I'll act at school, at home, and in the world. Sometimes those decisions are obvious and easy, but other times I struggle to choose wisely. I thank You that when someone asked You what the most important commandment was—what rule could guide our faithful living—You spoke it plainly: Love God with heart, soul, mind, and strength. That helps me know how to honor You and others with my feelings, spirit, mind, and body. Thank You for Your clear Word. Amen.

THINK ABOUT IT:
Are you facing a decision today that can be guided by what Jesus calls the most important commandment?

An Unlikely Choice

When Jesus reached the spot, he looked up and said to him, "Zacchaeus, come down immediately. I must stay at your house today." So he came down at once and welcomed him gladly. All the people saw this and began to mutter, "He has gone to be the guest of a sinner."
LUKE 19:5–7

When I think about who I spend time with, I know what kind of people religious folks think are the "right kind." And yet when I trace Your life in the Gospels, Jesus, I see that You surprised everyone with Your social choices! In fact, You chose the guy who was despised in town because of how he treated everyone. You handpicked the one whom everyone else tried to avoid. Give me Your spirit of generosity and kindness as I engage with others, so that I may learn to love like You loved. Amen.

THINK ABOUT IT:
Is there someone others avoid at school whom you could spend time with?

My Plans and God's Plans

The heart of man plans his way,
but the Lord establishes his steps.
Proverbs 16:9 esv

Father, so much of what I'm doing right now—especially in school—is about preparing for my future. But I have no idea what my life will look like a few years from now! It's as if I'm training for a race whose course I can't yet see. But today I know I can trust that my future is in Your hands. Even though I can't predict what college I might attend, what course of study I'll eventually choose, or what type of work I might one day perform, I am sure of one thing: You are with me today, and You'll be with me in all my tomorrows. God, today I simply commit my way to You, trusting that You are the One who will continue to guide me. Amen.

THINK ABOUT IT:
When you think about the future,
what makes you anxious?

....

....

....

....

....

....

....

....

Signs Of The Kingdom

Jesus replied, "Go back and report to John what you hear and see: The blind receive sight, the lame walk, those who have leprosy are cleansed, the deaf hear, the dead are raised, and the good news is proclaimed to the poor."
MATTHEW 11:4–5

God, I know John the Baptist's big assignment from You, his mission, was to prepare the way for the Messiah. So when he asked if You were "the one," You knew he'd *know* if his friends reported back what they knew of Your ministry. As I join Your work today, I believe the same is still true! You give sight to the blind. You heal the lame. You cleanse the diseased. You give hearing to the deaf. You raise the dead. You proclaim good news to the poor. Lord, show me how I can join You in what You're up to in the world today. Amen.

THINK ABOUT IT:
Is there a way in which God has asked you to join the transforming work of Jesus?

There Jesus Prayed

*Rising very early in the morning, while it
was still dark, he departed and went out
to a desolate place, and there he prayed.*
MARK 1:35 ESV

Father, I have felt a tug in my heart to carve out time to spend alone with You. But I confess that I often convince myself I'm too busy. That other things are more important. That I already know what the Bible says. That I don't really need to talk to You or hear from You. Forgive me. Thank You for the witness of Jesus, who shows me life that really is life. I notice Jesus' commitment to be alone with You, to be fed by You, and I long for the same. Meet me as I come to You. Amen.

THINK ABOUT IT:
*When is the best time of day for you to
make space to spend quietly with God?*

Abiding In Jesus' Love

By this my Father is glorified, that you bear much fruit and so prove to be my disciples. As the Father has loved me, so have I loved you. Abide in my love.
JOHN 15:8–9 ESV

Lord Jesus, I'm convinced that my Father, and Yours, has chosen me, called me, and sent me out to bear fruit in the world He loves. And to do that faithfully, I keep my eyes on You. I watch You talking to people, listening to people, showing God's love to those around You. And I see that in Your ministry You were *fueled* by Your Father's love. I'm blown away by Your assurance that You love me the same way the Father loved *You!* Jesus, I choose to abide in Your love. In fruitful seasons and in dry ones, I rest in You. Amen.

THINK ABOUT IT:
Can you close your eyes and picture what it looks like to abide in Jesus' love for you? What do you see?

....

....

....

....

....

....

....

....

I Sought You, And You Answered

I sought the LORD, and he answered me;
he delivered me from all my fears.
PSALM 34:4

God, Your Word assures me that You are near. You're close when I'm in my room. You're by my side when I'm on the way to school. You're near when I'm out shopping. Wherever I am, You're as close to me as my own skin! Yet the voice of the deceiver tries to convince me that I am alone—that You do not see me, You do not hear me, You do not answer me. Thank You for Your Word that assures me: when I seek You, You answer. You are a faithful Deliverer. So speak to the ears of my heart. Make Your voice plain to me—through Your Word, through other people, and in the stillness of my heart. I am listening. Amen.

THINK ABOUT IT:
How do you most often discern
God's voice speaking to you?

Wrapped In God's Love

*I am convinced that neither death nor life, neither angels
nor demons, neither the present nor the future, nor any
powers, neither height nor depth, nor anything else in all
creation, will be able to separate us from the love
of God that is in Christ Jesus our Lord.*
ROMANS 8:38–39

Lord, You know how the enemy tries to mess with me. He whispers that I am alone. He hisses that You do not care for me. He insists that I am unloved. But Your Spirit helps me recognize and reject those lies. Not only am I loved by You, but there is nothing on this earth—or beyond this earth!—that can separate me from Your love. Lord, on difficult days, this assurance helps me! I'm convinced that nothing can make me less loved by You. Amen.

THINK ABOUT IT:
*Can you describe a moment when you
knew, beyond a shadow of a doubt,
that you were deeply loved by God?*

Loving Others More Than Myself

*Love must be sincere. Hate what is evil; cling to
what is good. Be devoted to one another in love.
Honor one another above yourselves.*
ROMANS 12:9–10

God, You know how I am—how I naturally think of myself before others. That's my standard setting, but You are transforming me to be more like You. God, I want to love people the way You love people. I want those around me to know that I am *devoted* to them in love. Teach me what it looks like to honor others above myself, to love them more than I love myself. Open my mind to the small and big ways I can practice radical love for others: at the dinner table, at the grocery store, in my English class, at the bus stop, and at the mall. Today I commit myself to loving others well, in Your name. Amen.

THINK ABOUT IT:
*What is one way, this week, that you can
put the needs of others above your own?*

Seeking Treasure

Indeed, if you call out for insight and cry aloud for understanding, and if you look for it as for silver and search for it as for hidden treasure, then you will understand the fear of the LORD and find the knowledge of God.
PROVERBS 2:3–5

God, teach me to invest in what matters most. I confess that I squander my time, money, and energy on entertainment, on stuff I don't need, on useless distractions. And none satisfy the deep longings of my heart. So instead, I am choosing to seek insight and understanding, knowledge of You, the way explorers search for hidden treasure. And I thank You for Your promise that when I hunt for You, when I seek after You, I will find You! You are the treasure, and You will make Yourself known to me. Open my eyes to see Your face and my ears to hear Your voice. Amen.

THINK ABOUT IT:
Where is the place in your home where you cozy up to connect with God?

....

....

....

....

....

....

....

Teach Me To Pray

*Jesus was praying in a certain place, and when he finished,
one of his disciples said to him, "Lord, teach us to pray."*
LUKE 11:1 ESV

Lord Jesus, when I close my eyes and imagine You with Your friends, Your disciples, I can almost see Your face when one of them asks You to teach them to pray. And I think You surely must have smiled! You were delighted to teach Your friends to talk with Your Father, and theirs. Jesus, their request is mine. Teach me to pray. As I pray the Lord's Prayer, which You taught them, help me make the words my own. Teach me how to bring all my praise, all my concerns, all my sins, all my requests, and all my thanks to the feet of our Father. Amen.

THINK ABOUT IT:

*Do you ever pray the Lord's Prayer outside
of church, when you're speaking to God alone?*

Hair, Jewelry, And Fashion

Do not let your adorning be external—the braiding of hair and the putting on of gold jewelry, or the clothing you wear— but let your adorning be the hidden person of the heart with the imperishable beauty of a gentle and quiet spirit, which in God's sight is very precious.
1 PETER 3:3–4 ESV

God, so many voices, outlets, and platforms in my world seem to shout that my hair, jewelry, and clothing are what define me and other girls my age. It's obvious that the world values external beauty in girls and in women. I find such relief in Your reminder that my identity in You is secure no matter what I look like or what I wear. In Your eyes, I am accepted exactly as I am. And I resolve today to cultivate a spirit that delights Your heart. Thank You for the deep confidence and security I have in You. Amen.

THINK ABOUT IT:
What is one choice you can make today to cultivate the kind of beauty God treasures?

He Provides A Way

No temptation has overtaken you that is not common to man.
God is faithful, and he will not let you be tempted beyond
your ability, but with the temptation he will also provide the
way of escape, that you may be able to endure it.
1 CORINTHIANS 10:13 ESV

God, thank You that the temptations I face are no surprise to You. You know the ways the enemy tries to lure me, and You know my particular weaknesses. Not only do You *know*, but Your Word promises that You are my Helper. In every situation, You provide a way out, or You provide a way through. God, because I can't trust in my own strength, I put my confidence in You. And I'm keeping my eyes open for the way You will provide—helping me to escape the situation or giving me the strength to endure it. Thank You for Your grace and mercy. Amen.

THINK ABOUT IT:
For what recurring temptation
can you seek God's help?

God Intends Good

Joseph said to them, "Don't be afraid. Am I in the place of God? You intended to harm me, but God intended it for good to accomplish what is now being done, the saving of many lives."
GENESIS 50:19–20

God, when I look at some of the things that have happened in my life, I think about all that Jacob's son Joseph faced: he was betrayed by his family; he was sold into slavery; he was imprisoned. And yet You used those unique *unwanted* circumstances to shape Joseph's character. In every circumstance, he remained faithful to You and depended on You. Lord, I don't understand everything I've had to go through, any more than Joseph did. But like him, I turn my face toward You. I look to You for wisdom, and I depend on You for strength. Help me be Your faithful servant today. Amen.

THINK ABOUT IT:
Can you see the way a circumstance you wouldn't have chosen has been transformed by God?

....

....

....

....

....

....

....

....

It Is Written. . .

The devil said to him, "If you are the Son of God, tell this stone to become bread." Jesus answered, "It is written: 'Man shall not live on bread alone.'"
LUKE 4:3–4

Although the details of Jesus' temptation in the wilderness by the devil are so different from my life today, Lord, I am nourished by the truth I find there. Because I also hear the enemy challenging me to be my own boss; to ignore Your voice, to take matters into my own hands so I can get what I want. And I confess that I'm tempted to do that. But I recognize power in Jesus' words, "Man shall not live on bread alone." Jesus found strength by listening to Your voice when He was weakest. God, feed me with Your Word and give me the single-mindedness of Jesus to resist temptation. Amen.

THINK ABOUT IT:
As you consider the temptation that you battle most often, what scripture is God giving you to strengthen you to resist it?

....

....

....

....

....

....

....

A Compassionate Father

"He got up and went to his father. But while he was still a long way off, his father saw him and was filled with compassion for him; he ran to his son, threw his arms around him and kissed him."
LUKE 15:20

Lord, I confess I can be tempted to believe that You are judging me, that You are angry with me, or that You are disappointed in me. And yet that's not what I see in the face of Jesus, and it's not what I hear in His words. Instead, when He describes a stubborn, sinful kid like me who returns home after partying and blowing his dad's money, I recognize something different. I see Your face radiating compassion. I feel Your strong arms and Your joyful kiss. And I notice that You *delight* in Your children. Father, help me to see You through the eyes of Jesus. Amen.

THINK ABOUT IT:
*When you close your eyes and look toward God,
are you able to see a gracious face?*

Bearing Faithful Witness

"O Nebuchadnezzar, we have no need to answer you in this matter. If this be so, our God whom we serve is able to deliver us from the burning fiery furnace, and he will deliver us out of your hand, O king. But if not, be it known to you, O king, that we will not serve your gods or worship the golden image that you have set up."
DANIEL 3:16–18 ESV

Holy God, daily I notice the ways that I am being squeezed by the culture around me. I feel the pressures to speak, dress, and behave according to the world's values, not Yours. And yet in Your Word I see Your people bravely and boldly living lives that are faithful to You. Empower me today with the courage of Daniel and his friends, so that I might be a faithful witness to You, the one true God. Amen.

THINK ABOUT IT:
*What are the ways God is inviting you
to live counterculturally this week?*

I Know His Voice

"When he has brought out all his own, he goes on ahead of them, and his sheep follow him because they know his voice. But they will never follow a stranger; in fact, they will run away from him because they do not recognize a stranger's voice."

JOHN 10:4–5

Lord, thank You that You are the Good Shepherd. You feed Your sheep, and You feed me. You protect Your flock from wolves, and You protect me. You tenderly care for young lambs, and You care for me. And when You speak to me— through Your Word, through people who know and love You, through prayer—I recognize the sound of Your voice! Because I know You, because I'm learning what You're like in the person of Jesus, I can hear and discern Your voice. God, thank You. I'm listening. Amen.

THINK ABOUT IT:
Where is the most reliable place for you to encounter God's voice?

God, Show Me My Heart

Search me, God, and know my heart; test me and know my anxious thoughts. See if there is any offensive way in me, and lead me in the way everlasting.
PSALM 139:23–24

Father God, You know my heart. You know that I long to live a life that is pleasing to You. And You also know the ways I fall short—even in ways that I don't yet recognize! God, I confess that I'm often tempted to justify what I *want* to do: spending money, or watching that movie, or trying that activity, or stretching the truth about that one thing. And because I'm human, I need You to search my heart and show me those places. Help me to see the areas where You are calling me to be faithful, and give me the courage to obey. Amen.

THINK ABOUT IT:
*Right now, are you aware of an area
of sin that God is showing you?*

....

....

....

....

....

....

....

....

....

....

Faith In The Master

She came and knelt before him, saying, "Lord, help me."
And he answered, "It is not right to take the children's
bread and throw it to the dogs." She said, "Yes, Lord,
yet even the dogs eat the crumbs that fall from their
masters' table." Then Jesus answered her, "O woman,
great is your faith! Be it done for you as you desire."
MATTHEW 15:25–28 ESV

Jesus, in a story about this passionate woman who wasn't even a Jew, I learn about You and Your character. Although she was not in "the club," she believed that You were powerful. That You were gracious. That You could help her. And You saw her, You heard her, and You helped her by healing her daughter. God, give me this tenacity and determination when I pray, because You are worthy of my confidence. Amen.

THINK ABOUT IT:
Is there a situation in your life right now for which you
are praying desperately and doggedly to the Father?

What Real Love Looks Like

Love is patient and kind; love does not envy or boast; it is not arrogant or rude. It does not insist on its own way; it is not irritable or resentful; it does not rejoice at wrongdoing, but rejoices with the truth. Love bears all things, believes all things, hopes all things, endures all things.
1 CORINTHIANS 13:4–7 ESV

God, I confess that too many love songs and romantic comedies have shaped some of what I believe about love! Noticing where that falls short, I turn my eyes and ears to Your Word. Whether it is my love for my family, my love for my friends, my love for a boy, or my love for a world in need, You show me what *true* love is like. It's patient. Kind. Humble. Considerate. Generous. Righteous. Truthful. God, teach me to love the way You love in a way that reflects Your character. Amen.

THINK ABOUT IT:
Is there a difficult relationship in your life that requires the kind of real love Paul describes?

The Comfort I've Received From God

Blessed be the God and Father of our Lord Jesus Christ, the Father of mercies and God of all comfort, who comforts us in all our affliction, so that we may be able to comfort those who are in any affliction, with the comfort with which we ourselves are comforted by God.

2 Corinthians 1:3–4 esv

God, when I am afflicted—when I'm sad, when I'm lonely, when I'm suffering, when I'm undone emotionally—You are near. You do not run from me, but You comfort me in Your loving arms. And because You've comforted me in the past, I know how to care for others who are also in need. God, open my eyes to those who are hurting, so that I might demonstrate the comfort, the patience, and the generous love that You've offered to me. Amen.

THINK ABOUT IT:

How might you comfort someone in your life who is suffering in ways that are similar to what you have endured?

You Must Go

"Alas, Sovereign Lord," I said, "I do not know how to speak; I am too young." But the Lord said to me, "Do not say, 'I am too young.' You must go to everyone I send you to and say whatever I command you. Do not be afraid of them, for I am with you and will rescue you," declares the Lord.

JEREMIAH 1:6–8

Thank You, Lord, for the witness of Jeremiah. He was young like me when You called him. He wasn't confident that he had the skills to speak on Your behalf. But Your words to him are also Your words to me, "You must go to everyone I send you to and say whatever I command you." Lord, although it's scary, I know I can trust in You. Give me the boldness of Jeremiah to say *yes* when You call. Amen.

THINK ABOUT IT:
When has God called you to do something that is more than you felt capable of doing in your own strength?

Presenting My Requests To God

Do not be anxious about anything, but in every situation, by prayer and petition, with thanksgiving, present your requests to God. And the peace of God, which transcends all understanding, will guard your hearts and your minds in Christ Jesus.
PHILIPPIANS 4:6–7

God, You know what's in my heart. You know the things I worry about. You notice when I feel anxious. You pay attention when I'm afraid. And Your Word promises me that I can offer my worries, my anxiety, and my fears to You. And when I do, I know that You are faithful to fill me with Your peace that passes understanding. So I'm handing over everything that's weighing down my heart, and I trust that You care. Receive my concerns and grant me Your peace. Amen.

THINK ABOUT IT:
Is there a particular worry that God's Spirit is welcoming you to release today?

Faith That's Pure

Religion that God our Father accepts as pure and faultless is this: to look after orphans and widows in their distress and to keep oneself from being polluted by the world.
JAMES 1:27

Lord, although You are powerful, You care for the weak. And although You are famous, You love the forgotten. And I learn in Your Word that You expect Your people to do the same. God, I'm reminded that just as there were desperate widows and orphans in the first century, there are so many with desperate needs today. Whether it's a woman who's been forgotten in a local nursing home, or a classmate in foster care who's lost his parents, open my eyes to notice the ones You are inviting me to love. Amen.

THINK ABOUT IT:
Who is the weak or vulnerable person near you whom God is inviting you to love in His name?

Sharing My "More Than Enough"

Suppose someone has enough to live and sees a brother or sister in need, but does not help. Then God's love is not living in that person. My children, we should love people not only with words and talk, but by our actions and true caring.
1 JOHN 3:17–18 NCV

God, You have met all my needs. And yet I confess that I do see people in need but fail to help them. I've seen kids getting picked on at school or on the bus. I've seen folks asking for food or money or a job on the street corner. If I'm honest, I even know what kind of help my parents and siblings need at home. But too often I choose my own comfort over the needs of others. Forgive me, Lord. Show me one thing I can do this week to meet the needs of another. Amen.

THINK ABOUT IT:
What is one need God has shown you that you have the ability to meet?

....

....

....

....

....

....

....

....

....

Be Still

He says, "Be still, and know that I am God; I will be exalted
among the nations, I will be exalted in the earth."
PSALM 46:10

Lord, You know that when my feet hit the ground in the
morning, I can be in constant motion until my head hits the
pillow at night. And yet I long to find rest in You. So I thank
You that Your gentle voice whispers to my heart, *Be still, and
know that I am God*. Today I choose to be still before You.
To shut off my phone. To pull out my earbuds. To close my
mouth. And to set the eyes and ears of my heart on You.
Father, give me the discipline to rest in the peace You give
so freely. Amen.

THINK ABOUT IT:
*What things—inside of you and outside of you—
do you need to "shut off" in order to be still before God?*

Jesus Makes The Father Known

No one has ever seen God, but the one and only Son,
who is himself God and is in closest relationship
with the Father, has made him known.
JOHN 1:18

Father, You know that the great desire of my heart is to see You, to hear You, to know You, to love You. And yet I cannot experience You with my physical eyes and ears. But You have shared with me the *secret* of recognizing Your face, Your voice, and Your loving presence. Because I recognize You, I know You through the person of Jesus. In His countenance, I see Your face. In His words, I hear Your voice. And in His actions, I recognize Your ways. Thank You for revealing Yourself clearly through the person of Jesus. Help me to recognize You today. Amen.

THINK ABOUT IT:
When was a time you recognized God
the Father through the person of Jesus?

All Have Sinned

*All have sinned and fall
short of the glory of God.*
ROMANS 3:23

Lord, I confess that when I read Your Word, I am quick to recognize the sin of others: their gossip, their pride, their self-centeredness, their unkindness. For some reason, when I look at my own life, I'm slower to recognize *my* sin. I minimize it. I ignore it. I rationalize it. And yet Your Word reminds me that I am no different from anyone else. I am a sinner, and I fall short of Your good intentions for me and my life. Forgive me. Help me to see clearly the ways I miss the mark You have set, and after I confess my sin to You, help me live a life that really is life. Amen.

THINK ABOUT IT:
*Is there a particular sin that you are most
often tempted to ignore in your own life?*

....

....

....

....

....

....

....

....

....

Nothing Can Separate Me From God's Love

Who shall separate us from the love of Christ?
Shall trouble or hardship or persecution or
famine or nakedness or danger or sword?
ROMANS 8:35

Jesus, You know that when I'm suffering, when I'm in trouble, when I'm in need, and when I'm in danger, I have difficulty recognizing how near You are to me. When I struggle, it's harder for me to notice Your presence and Your love. And when my mind makes up stories that are not true, I accept the lie that You are not with me and You are not for me. And yet Your Word says that nothing—not one thing on heaven or on earth—can separate me from Your love. Knit the reality of that transforming truth into my heart today, in Jesus' name. Amen.

THINK ABOUT IT:
What situation in your life makes it most
difficult for you to experience God's love?

....

....

....

....

....

....

....

....

He Is My Fortress

Truly my soul finds rest in God; my salvation comes
from him. Truly he is my rock and my salvation;
he is my fortress, I will never be shaken.
PSALM 62:1–2

Lord, I am so used to feeling vulnerable and alone that I can feel so far from You. But Your Word promises that You are all the shelter and protection I need: You are my rock; You are my fortress. Because You are unshakable, You are a safe refuge for me. In the shelter of Your protection, I set up camp and make a home with You. You swaddle me like a baby, and You care for me. Lord, in Your presence I am secure, I am held, I am loved. Thank You for being my Protector. Amen.

THINK ABOUT IT:
When do you feel most vulnerable and
in need of God's mighty protection?

....

....

....

....

....

....

....

....

Casting My Anxieties Onto God

Humble yourselves, therefore, under the mighty hand of God so that at the proper time he may exalt you, casting all your anxieties on him, because he cares for you.
1 PETER 5:6–7 ESV

God, You know every one of the anxieties, big and small, that I carry in my heart. You know the social situations that stress me out. You know the ways I worry about my family, near and far. You know how I worry about school and my future. And You even know the smaller anxieties I carry, like competing in athletics and other activities, winning the approval of others, and looking the way I think I should look. I thank You that You see, You notice, and You care. God, confident that You cherish me, today I cast every anxiety in my heart on You. Receive them and set me free. Amen.

THINK ABOUT IT:
Is there a niggling worry that you've carried for too long?

How I Treat Others

*In everything, do to others what you would have them
do to you, for this sums up the Law and the Prophets.*
MATTHEW 7:12

God, although knowing, loving, and serving You takes everything I have, You have really made it pretty simple: You ask me to do to others what I'd want them to do to me. That guide actually helps me! When I'm deciding how to respond to my sibling who's asking for a favor, I will think of what I'd want her to do for me. When I speak to my parents, especially when I'm upset, I will speak to them the way I'd want them to speak to me. When I'm with my friends—and even my enemies!—I'll treat them the way I'd want to be treated. Equip me to love others the way You love me. Amen.

THINK ABOUT IT:
*When is it hardest to treat others the
way you'd want to be treated?*

....

....

....

....

....

....

....

....

Giving Thanks To Him

Enter his gates with thanksgiving and his courts with praise; give thanks to him and praise his name. For the LORD is good and his love endures forever; his faithfulness continues through all generations.
PSALM 100:4–5

Lord, You are good. Your love endures forever, and Your faithfulness continues through all generations. Because of who You are, God, I give You thanks and praise. Yet I confess that gratitude isn't always the first thing in my heart! I'm tempted to notice what's negative, what I don't have, what I want. And yet the psalmist joyfully invites me to be grateful. Today I give You thanks for all Your good gifts to me: my family, my church, my friends, my education, my safe home, and of course for all the ways You meet my daily needs. Today I practice gratitude. Amen.

THINK ABOUT IT:
What do you most often thank God for?
What are you less likely to thank God for?

Transform Me

*"I tell you that anyone who is angry with a brother
or sister will be subject to judgment. Again, anyone
who says to a brother or sister, 'Raca,' is answerable
to the court. And anyone who says, 'You fool!'
will be in danger of the fire of hell."*
MATTHEW 5:22

God, You know me inside and out. You hear the ugly or un-kind words that carelessly slip out of my mouth, and You know the ones I harbor in my heart. And Jesus's words remind me that *You care*. God, transform my heart, my mind, and my speech, so that I might be gracious and generous toward others. When I look at my neighbor, a fellow student, a person with a disability, or a person living on the street, may I see what You see in each one. Amen.

THINK ABOUT IT:
*Who is the person, or the people,
you are most likely to treat unkindly?*

I Am Yours

When all the people were being baptized, Jesus was baptized too. And as he was praying, heaven was opened and the Holy Spirit descended on him in bodily form like a dove. And a voice came from heaven: "You are my Son, whom I love; with you I am well pleased."
LUKE 3:21–22

Father, thank You that I can listen in on Your conversation with Your Son. When I close my eyes, I can hear Your gracious voice speaking the words over Jesus that were, and are, most true about His identity. As I quiet my heart, I listen for Your voice speaking the truth of *my* identity: calling me Your daughter, affirming Your love, announcing Your delight in me. Like Jesus, I belong to You. Amen.

THINK ABOUT IT:
When you listen for God's voice speaking to your heart about the truth of your identity, what do you hear?

Bread That Truly Satisfies

"I am the living bread that came down from heaven. Whoever eats this bread will live forever. This bread is my flesh, which I will give for the life of the world."
JOHN 6:51

Lord, You know how I am tempted to fill myself with things that do not truly satisfy. I feast on social media, binge on music, eat to my heart's content, and keep my shopping cart full. I fill my eyes, my ears, my stomach, and my closet, but I still feel empty. Jesus, I choose instead to feast on You. Live in me so that I might be fueled by Your life. Feed me, fill me, and use me, for the glory of Your kingdom. You are the Bread that feeds a world in need. Amen.

THINK ABOUT IT:
What are the ways that you are being filled by the body and life of Jesus?

Loving As Jesus Loved

*Greater love has no one than this: to lay
down one's life for one's friends. You are
my friends if you do what I command.*
JOHN 15:13–14

God, the word *love* is thrown around in so many ways: I *love*
chocolate; I *love* my grandma; I *love* romantic comedies; I
love *You!* (And, of course, there are the romantic feelings in
my heart!) But each of those is different from the way You
love. And I know what real love is only by seeing Your love at
work in the life of Jesus. When I see Jesus loving His friends,
sacrificing His life for them, I understand how to love well.
God, teach me how to love others well, even at cost to myself. Amen.

THINK ABOUT IT:

*What are the kinds of sacrifices
you have made for people you love?
And how have they sacrificed for you?*

A Light Has Dawned

*The people walking in darkness have seen
a great light; on those living in the land
of deep darkness a light has dawned.*
ISAIAH 9:2

God, You have come to Your people as a light in the darkness. You created the sun in the sky. You opened the eyes of the Israelites to see You and know You. And You came to us, as the Light of the World, in the person of Jesus. And just as You shone in the world, I welcome Your light to reign in my heart. Where there are shadows of sin, shine Your light and dispel the darkness. Where there are dark chambers of pain, I want You to shine Your healing light. God, I welcome Your light to dawn in all my dark places, so that I might be filled with Your light. Amen.

THINK ABOUT IT:
*Is there place in your heart that
is in need of God's light today?*

Bearing Faithful Witness

Godliness with contentment is great gain, for we brought nothing into the world, and we cannot take anything out of the world. But if we have food and clothing, with these we will be content.
1 TIMOTHY 6:6–8 ESV

Faithful Provider, I am grateful that You have given me all that I need. You've provided food for my stomach, clothing for my body, and a pillow for my head. Thank You. And yet the ads that bombard me scream that I need more, that I deserve more. I confess that I am tempted to believe the hype. And yet I know that it is untrue. What is most true is that You are my Good Shepherd who provides everything I need. Thank You, Father. Amen.

THINK ABOUT IT:

What are some of the ways the world tries to trigger your desires for more than you need?

Your Sheep Know Your Voice

The sheep hear his voice, and he calls his own sheep by name and leads them out. When he has brought out all his own, he goes before them, and the sheep follow him, for they know his voice.
JOHN 10:3–4 ESV

Lord, You've made Yourself known to us as a Shepherd who is good. And I do believe that Your sheep know the sound of Your voice. I'm one of those lambs You've redeemed. So today I tilt my ear toward You. I listen for the words You speak in scripture. I listen for the ways You are speaking to me through others. I listen for the times You whisper Your truth to my heart. Speak, Lord, because I'm listening. Give me courage to respond in faith to You. Amen.

THINK ABOUT IT:
*How do you most often
hear God speaking to you?*

Perfect Love Drives Out Fear

We know and rely on the love God has for us. God is love.
Whoever lives in love lives in God, and God in them. . . .
There is no fear in love. But perfect love drives out fear,
because fear has to do with punishment. The one
who fears is not made perfect in love.
1 JOHN 4:16, 18

God, Your Word reminds me that love and fear are incompatible. And *You are love.* So wherever You are, fear has no place. Your love drives it out. Help me to hold this assurance in my heart today. When I begin to feel afraid, I ask You to fill my entire body with Your love. I rely on You today to displace any fear in my heart. Thank You for the great love You have for me, in Jesus' name. Amen.

THINK ABOUT IT:
When do you notice fear taking up space in your
heart? Can you close your eyes and see God's
love physically and spiritually displacing fear?

Having No Other Gods

"You shall have no other gods before me. You shall not make for yourself an image in the form of anything in heaven above or on the earth beneath or in the waters below. You shall not bow down to them or worship them; for I, the LORD your God, am a jealous God."
EXODUS 20:3–5

Lord, I beg You to teach me, from Your Word, more about You and more about me. Because I don't make or trust in handmade idols, it's tempting to think Your ancient command is for someone else. But Your Spirit opens my eyes to the ways in which I put my trust in other sources of security: in numbers of "likes," in my performance, in my reputation, in my popularity, and in anything else that makes me feel secure. Forgive me. Teach me today what it means to have no other gods before You. Amen.

THINK ABOUT IT:
When you ask God to show you how you're tempted to seek false security, what does God say?

I Have Seen It

That which was from the beginning, which we have heard,
which we have seen with our eyes, which we have looked
at and our hands have touched—this we proclaim
concerning the Word of life. The life appeared.
1 JOHN 1:1–2

God, You have done mighty wonders in Your world and in my life. Yet I hear voices in culture that mock You, suggesting that You do not exist, or that You are weak. So I thank You for the powerful witness to You that I've experienced. I've heard the true words that have been passed down through the generations. With my eyes I've seen Your work in my life and in the lives of others. And I believe the earliest witnesses who touched You with their hands! You are the source of life, and I will trust You today. Amen.

THINK ABOUT IT:

What is the most persuasive evidence you've
seen of God's great love for the world?

When I'm Tempted

When tempted, no one should say, "God is tempting me."
For God cannot be tempted by evil, nor does he tempt
anyone; but each person is tempted when they are
dragged away by their own evil desire and enticed.
JAMES 1:13–14

Father God, You know my heart. And You know the unique temptations I face—the ways I'm enticed, daily, to choose my way over Your way. It starts with my small choices, and then when I feed my desires they seem to snowball, gaining power. Forgive me. I agree that You are not the author of temptation. Rather, when I get dragged away by sin, it is because I've agreed to it. Strengthen me today to resist evil. Teach me to rely on Your Spirit in every moment. Amen.

THINK ABOUT IT:
Is there a particular circumstance that God's Spirit
nudges you to avoid in order to resist temptation?

....

....

....

....

....

....

....

....

Praying For My Leaders

I urge, then, first of all, that petitions, prayers,
intercession and thanksgiving be made for all people—
for kings and all those in authority, that we may live
peaceful and quiet lives in all godliness and holiness.
1 TIMOTHY 2:1–2

God, when I look around the world You love, I see so much divisiveness and conflict. Nations war against nations, and even within my own country, political parties wage war against one another. And while it's tempting to get my two cents in on social media, or in conversations with enemies and friends, You describe a better way. Knowing how we are, You instruct us—instruct *me*—to pray for those who are in authority. Most of the time I don't want to, but I submit to You, God. This day I pray that You will guide those in authority so that the world You love can enjoy peace. Amen.

THINK ABOUT IT:
Which leader—local, national, or international—
do you have the most difficulty bringing to God in prayer?

....

....

....

....

....

....

....

Jesus Has Compassion On Me

Jesus called his disciples to him and said, "I have compassion on the crowd because they have been with me now three days and have nothing to eat. And I am unwilling to send them away hungry, lest they faint on the way."
MATTHEW 15:32 ESV

It is a gift, Jesus, to see the way You interacted with tired, hungry folks who were so much like me. And I notice that You were concerned about people's hearts, minds, and bodies. You fed them with Your words, and then You fed them with bread. And You do the same today. Thank You that You notice my needs as well. I trust that You know what I need and are my Good Provider today. Amen.

THINK ABOUT IT:
Beyond the hunger in your belly, what is one hunger you are asking Jesus to fill?

Being A Good Steward Of Grace

As each has received a gift, use it to serve one another,
as good stewards of God's varied grace: whoever speaks,
as one who speaks oracles of God; whoever serves, as one
who serves by the strength that God supplies—in order
that in everything God may be glorified.
1 PETER 4:10–11 ESV

God, I am grateful for the unique gifts You have given me.
Thanks that I have a unique set of gifts that are meant to
glorify You and serve others. And so I offer back to You the
gifts I've been given: eyes that discern, a tongue that speaks,
a heart that loves, hands that create, arms that serve, and
legs that move toward others. Show me how I can share the
gifts You've given with the world You love. Amen.

THINK ABOUT IT:
When you think of two or three gifts God has
given you, how can you see yourself using
those on behalf of the world God loves?

Listening for God's Voice

The LORD came and stood, calling as at other times, "Samuel! Samuel!" And Samuel said, "Speak, for your servant hears."
1 SAMUEL 3:10 ESV

Gracious God, I long to be used by You for the building of Your kingdom. And I notice, in Your Word, that You call, empower, and use unlikely servants like me. When You called Samuel, he was just a boy! So with Samuel I say, "Speak, Lord, for your servant is listening." God, I am listening to Your Word, to Your still, small voice in prayer, and to the guiding words of those who love You. I believe that You still call and use those who aren't quite adults, and I believe that You are using me. I'm listening. Amen.

THINK ABOUT IT:

Can you think of a time when you knew that God had prompted or nudged you to act in obedience to Him?

....

....

....

....

....

....

....

....

....

Always Full Of Grace

Be wise in the way you act toward outsiders; make the most of every opportunity. Let your conversation be always full of grace, seasoned with salt, so that you may know how to answer everyone.

COLOSSIANS 4:5–6

Lord, I thank You that I am surrounded by other believers—godly people who know You, love You, and want to serve You. But You've also called me to be salt and light in the world, and that means spending time with those who don't know You. God, teach me how to behave among them. Give me Your grace so that I might faithfully represent You and draw others into Your family. I trust that You are guiding and leading me as I seek to honor You. Amen.

THINK ABOUT IT:

Who is one person, who's not yet a believer, that God has put on your heart to love in His name?

Pressing On Toward The Goal

I press on toward the goal to win the prize for which God has called me heavenward in Christ Jesus.
PHILIPPIANS 3:14

God, when I think about my journey with You, I'm reminded of someone running a marathon who has never trained for it. I'll be running strong for a while—loving You with my whole heart, serving others—and then I'll fizzle out. I'll walk for a while and then be sidetracked by roadside distractions. You fuel me up with Your Word and Your presence, and I start jogging again. Lord, You know the ways I stumble, fall, and get back up again. Each time, Your Spirit renews my commitment to press on toward the goal to win the prize for which You've called me. Be my strength as I walk with You today, Lord. Amen.

THINK ABOUT IT:

When you are weary in your walk with God, how does He strengthen and sustain you?

Being Transformed By Scripture

All Scripture is God-breathed and is useful for teaching, rebuking, correcting and training in righteousness, so that the servant of God may be thoroughly equipped for every good work.
2 TIMOTHY 3:16–17

Lord, today I give You thanks for the Scriptures. You have been so gracious and kind to speak to human hearts through Your holy Word. I ask that Your Spirit would breathe in my heart as I read it so that I might be transformed. I want to learn. I am willing to be rebuked and corrected. And I am committed to being trained in righteousness so that I can be ready for anything You ask me to do. God, feed me with Your Word and strengthen me to respond to You in obedience. I want to be Your faithful servant. Amen.

THINK ABOUT IT:
What is God teaching you through His holy Word this week?

Forgiving Like I've Been Forgiven

*Peter came up and said to him, "Lord, how often
will my brother sin against me, and I forgive him?
As many as seven times?" Jesus said to him, "I do not
say to you seven times, but seventy-seven times."*
MATTHEW 18:21–22 ESV

Lord, when I hear Peter's question to You, I understand where he is coming from! You command us to forgive, and when I do, it always takes faith, energy, and courage. I forgive out of obedience to You and, in the end, it's my heart that is blessed and liberated. But that's the *first* time. When I have to forgive the same person again, I'm usually not feeling it. And by the seventh time? I am so over it. Although I don't want to, I receive Your call to forgive again and again and again. Help me forgive others as You've forgiven me. Amen.

THINK ABOUT IT:
*Who is one person God is inviting you
to forgive again and again and again?*

Giving All My Fear To God

*I, the L**ORD** your God, hold your right hand; it is I who say to you, "Fear not, I am the one who helps you."*
ISAIAH 41:13 ESV

God, I confess that some things in my life make me feel afraid. Anxious. Upset. I am grateful that You know the exact nature of each and every thought. And when I allow my mind to dwell on my worries, when I allow them to swirl through my mind, I feel undone. When I close my eyes, though, I see You holding my right hand. And I hear Your voice whispering to my heart, *Fear not.* Lord, thank You for being my Good Helper. Today I grasp Your hand and listen for Your voice. Amen.

THINK ABOUT IT:
What fears is God inviting you to release into His loving care?

Beloved By The Father

*See what great love the Father has
lavished on us, that we should be called
children of God! And that is what we are!*
1 JOHN 3:1

God, I thank You that You have called me Your daughter. And yet at times I still hear the lying whispers of the enemy, hissing words to my spirit like: *unwanted, forgotten, unattractive, unloved, abandoned*, and *not enough*. In the name of Jesus, I reject those lies of the enemy. You don't just love me because You have to, but You lavish abundant love on me! To You, I'm not a stranger. I'm not an orphan. I'm not a project. I am Your daughter. I belong to You, and You call me *beloved*. Father, this week help me to claim the truth of my belovedness and open my eyes to all the ways You are a gracious Father to me. Amen.

THINK ABOUT IT:
*What is one of the lies the enemy hisses to your
heart that you can replace with the word beloved?*

....

....

....

....

....

....

....

The Unlikely Way

"If anyone would come after me, let him deny himself and take up his cross and follow me. For whoever would save his life will lose it, but whoever loses his life for my sake and the gospel's will save it. For what does it profit a man to gain the whole world and forfeit his soul?"
MARK 8:34–37 ESV

Father, You know how I'm wired, and You know how I operate. Like most people, I naturally want to *save* my own life. I want my needs to be met. I want to enjoy pleasure. But when I look at Jesus, and when I listen to His words, I recognize another way. An *unlikely* way. A *better* way. *Your* way. Although I'm not a big fan of denying myself, teach me what it means to take up my cross and follow You. Be my Helper. Amen.

THINK ABOUT IT:
Is there a way in which God is asking you to sacrifice, to lose your life for His sake today?

....
....
....
....
....
....
....
....

Jesus Prays For Us

"Simon, Simon, behold, Satan demanded to have you, that he might sift you like wheat, but I have prayed for you that your faith may not fail."
Luke 22:31–32 esv

So many days, Lord, I forget that there is a battle being waged in the heavenly places. I ignore the real presence of the one who steals, kills, and destroys. And just as the enemy wanted to take down Simon Peter, he also has his sights set on me. But I am not afraid, because You are my Good Protector. And I'm encouraged that just as You prayed for Your friend Peter, You pray for me. You intercede to our Father on my behalf. Today my faith is strengthened by Your love and Your intercession for me. Amen.

THINK ABOUT IT:
How is the enemy trying to attack you in this season? And how are you seeing God's good protection?

God's Power, My Weakness

*A thorn was given me in the flesh, a messenger of
Satan to harass me, to keep me from becoming conceited.
Three times I pleaded with the Lord about this, that it
should leave me. But he said to me, "My grace is sufficient
for you, for my power is made perfect in weakness."*
2 Corinthians 12:7–9 esv

Lord, You know I'd rather be first than last. I'd rather be seen
than ignored. I'd rather be strong than weak. But when I look
at the lives of Your saints—Moses, Mary, Paul—I see that You
shone most brightly in their weaknesses. Even so, like Paul,
my preference would be for You to take away the thorns
in my life, the weaknesses, the hindrances. But I hear Your
voice soothing me and saying, "My power is made perfect in
weakness." May it be so for me today. Amen.

THINK ABOUT IT:
*Is there an area in your life where you are weak,
but where God can be seen as strong?*

Friends Forever

Two are better than one, because they have a good reward for their toil. For if they fall, one will lift up his fellow. But woe to him who is alone when he falls and has not another to lift him up!
ECCLESIASTES 4:9–10 ESV

I thank You, God, that You have placed me in a community of people who know You and love You. And I thank You especially for the friendships You have placed in my life. They are a good gift from You. God, teach me how to be the kind of friend who lifts others up. And when I am in need, strengthen my friends to do the same for me. Together, Lord, we will love one another and glorify You. Amen.

THINK ABOUT IT:
Can you think of one friend in your life who is able to support you as a Christian sister?

God's Love For Me

This is love: not that we loved God,
but that he loved us and sent his Son
as an atoning sacrifice for our sins.
1 JOHN 4:10

God, You know how earnestly I want to know You, love You, and serve You. When I'm at home, at church, at school, and out in the world, I try to honor You in all I do. But I confess that when I'm trying to *be* good and to *do* good, I can lose sight of what matters most. It's not that I love You, it's that *You loved me first.* You loved me so much that You sent Your Son to die for my sin. So today that is where I will begin— with Your love for me. And I'll go from there! I thank You in the strong name of Jesus. Amen.

THINK ABOUT IT:

What changes in your life when you live with
a full awareness of God's great love for you?

God Gives Me Words

*Pray also for me, that whenever I speak,
words may be given me so that I will fearlessly
make known the mystery of the gospel.*
EPHESIANS 6:19

Lord, thank You that You have chosen me to be Your beloved daughter. The security I have in Your love for me is the most important thing about who I am. But I confess that sometimes I am slow to share Your grace with others. I can be sheepish and shy when it comes to talking about You to those who don't know You. Forgive me. Your Word convinces me that whenever I open my mouth to share the mysteries of the Gospel, the words that come out are not even mine. They are Yours! So give me a willing spirit to share the good news of Your Gospel with others today for Your glory. Amen.

THINK ABOUT IT:
*Is there someone God is putting on your heart
who needs to hear about the love of Jesus?*

Walking By The Spirit Every Day

*Walk by the Spirit, and you will not
gratify the desires of the flesh.*
GALATIANS 5:16

Thank You, Lord, that I belong to You. You have redeemed me, once and for all. And yet each day, I am learning what it means to walk by Your Spirit. I'm discovering that I need to *choose* to be led by You. Part of that choice is refusing to gratify the desires of my flesh. So today I commit myself to walking in sync with You. I ask for Your help in rejecting all that would distract me from You and Your good purposes for my life. I release every want, yearning, hunger, and thought that is not from You. Today I am taking one step at a time by the power of Your Spirit. Amen.

THINK ABOUT IT:
*What desire of the flesh feels
the most demanding today?*

The Simple Way To Honor God

Do everything in love.
1 CORINTHIANS 16:14

God, You are showing me what it looks like to live a life that is patterned after the person of Jesus. Today that is the deepest desire of my heart. But You know that sometimes I try to make it harder than it should be! I create lists of rules, practices, behaviors, and hurdles I have to jump over to be like Jesus. But when I set my eyes on You and notice the way Jesus lived, I'm reminded that Your invitation to live well is simple: *do everything in love.* So that's my goal today. As I'm studying, as I'm talking to my friends at lunch, as I'm taking out the trash, as I'm tipping a waitress for her service: *help me to do everything in love.* Amen.

THINK ABOUT IT:
*What is going to look different in your life today
as you commit to doing everything in love?*

More Than A Conqueror

Who shall separate us from the love of Christ? Shall trouble or hardship or persecution or famine or nakedness or danger or sword?. . . . No, in all these things we are more than conquerors through him who loved us.
ROMANS 8:35, 37

Your Word reminds me, God, that You are with me in the "highs" of my life: when I came to know You, when I'm feeling loved by my family, when a special boy notices me, when I'm surrounded by my friends. But You are also near during the unavoidable "lows": when I'm in trouble, when I'm facing hardship, when I'm being persecuted. I am confident in this because I have seen You protect Your people when they faced famine, nakedness, danger, and sword. But they were conquerors in You, and I am as well. Nothing, in heaven or on earth, can separate me from Your love. Amen.

THINK ABOUT IT:
What situation in your life makes you feel as though God is far away?

Choosing What Is Best

The Lord answered her, "Martha, Martha, you are anxious and troubled about many things, but one thing is necessary. Mary has chosen the good portion, which will not be taken away from her."
LUKE 10:41–42 ESV

God, when I read about Mary and Martha, I recognize qualities in them that I see in myself. I know how peaceful and fulfilling it is to sit, like Mary, and soak in Your presence, gaze at Your face, and listen to Your words. But I also know what it is like to scramble around like Martha, trying to accomplish so much and maybe even feeling a little resentful that I'm not just sitting around like Mary. Check my heart, Lord. I see that the choice is mine, so help me choose what is best. Amen.

THINK ABOUT IT:
Are you more like Martha or like Mary?
How can you choose the good portion today?

Loving Those Who Are Hard To Love

Whoever claims to love God yet hates a brother or sister is a liar. For whoever does not love their brother and sister, whom they have seen, cannot love God, whom they have not seen. And he has given us this command: Anyone who loves God must also love their brother and sister.
1 JOHN 4:20–21

Lord, when I'm honest, I want to believe that I can love You and even love most people, but not *all* of them. There are some folks in my life who are just really hard to love! (You know exactly who I mean.) And many people are a bit beyond my orbit—the ones I see on the street or in the news; those who are poor, hungry, sick, or at war. I don't know how to love these people either. But You do know how to love them, Lord. So equip me to love those who are near and those who are far away with Your love. Amen.

THINK ABOUT IT:
Is there someone, near or far, whom God has been prompting you to love?

....

....

....

....

....

....

....

An Unlikely Plan

*David triumphed over the Philistine with a
sling and a stone; without a sword in his hand
he struck down the Philistine and killed him.*
1 SAMUEL 17:50

God, when I read Your Word, it becomes so clear that Your ways are not our ways. You use what is weak to shame the strong. When young David defeated the great giant Goliath, he didn't do it with the weapons of warriors. That boy did it with a toy! A slingshot! You chose David, who was weak, and You equipped him with what he needed to protect his people. God, I believe that, even though I'm young, You've called my name. You've invited me to serve You. And I trust that You'll give me whatever I need—words, skills, instincts, courage—to accomplish what You've called me to do. I trust that You will equip me. Amen.

THINK ABOUT IT:
*What is one "tool" God has given
you with which you can serve Him?*

fessing. . . Again

"we confess our sins, he is faithful and
just to forgive us our sins and to cleanse
us from all unrighteousness."
1 JOHN 1:9 ESV

God, I thank You that You know me inside and out, and that You love me. When I mess up, when I have to confess the *same thing* to You, on repeat, I imagine You must be tired of my sin. Tired of my prayers. But You promise in Your Word that if I confess, You're faithful to forgive and to cleanse me—not just once, but again and again. Lord, thank You for Your grace that is bigger than my imagination. Your willingness to hear my prayers, even though they're like the same playlist repeating again and again, is a good gift. Thank You for Your graciousness toward me every day. Amen.

THINK ABOUT IT:
*Is there a sin—or a sin "theme"—
that you confess to God repeatedly?*

Jesus' Prayer For Me

*I have made you known to them, and will continue to
make you known in order that the love you have for
me may be in them and that I myself may be in them.*
JOHN 17:26

Lord, I am so blessed that I get to overhear the prayers of
Jesus. I hear Him talking to You, Father. That blows me away.
It reminds me that Jesus was faithful in making You known.
And even as He neared death, He promised that He would
continue to make You known. Jesus' heart was that the love
You have for Him would be in Your people, would be in *me*.
And Jesus also promised to live in us and in *me*. Today I cling
to these words that Jesus prayed to You. May Your love and
the life of Jesus abide in me. Amen.

THINK ABOUT IT:
*What changes in you as you become aware
that God's love, and Jesus, reside within you?*

....

....

....

....

....

....

....

....

....

The Truth Is Setting Me Free

To the Jews who had believed him, Jesus said, "If you hold to my teaching, you are really my disciples. Then you will know the truth, and the truth will set you free."
JOHN 8:31–32

Lord, there have been seasons of my walk with You—like when I first came to know You—when I was on fire with passion for You. And there have been other seasons when I've felt weary. When I've lost my zeal for You. When my spirit has felt tired. That is why I am encouraged when I listen to Jesus' words to His followers. He promises that in this journey with You, we are empowered, liberated, and set free by Your truth. That's what I hold on to today. As I purpose to be Your faithful follower, I cling to Your truth and I'm revived by Your Word. Amen.

THINK ABOUT IT:
What truth from God's Word do you need to hold on to today?

Scripture Index